I AM MICHAEL ALAGO

I AM MICHAEL ALAGO

Breathing Music. Signing Metallica. Beating Death.

Michael Alago
with
Laura Davis-Chanin

Backbeat
Books

Guilford, Connecticut

Backbeat Books
An imprint of The Rowman & Littlefield Publishing Group, Inc.
4501 Forbes Blvd., Ste. 200
Lanham, MD 20706
www.rowman.com

Distributed by NATIONAL BOOK NETWORK

British Library Cataloguing in Publication Information Available

Library of Congress Cataloging-in-Publication Data Available

ISBN 978-1-6171-3725-9 (paperback)
ISBN 978-1-4930-5067-3 (e-book)

♾™ The paper used in this publication meets the minimum requirements of
American National Standard for Information Sciences—Permanence of Paper
for Printed Library Materials, ANSI/NISO Z39.48-1992.

This book is dedicated to my mother, Blanche,
with all the love I have in my heart

CONTENTS

FOREWORD

Mina Caputo—Vocalist and songwriter for Life of Agony

I Am Michael Alago is a delight to read. A victorious exercise in creative writing and reading in which diary entries, letters, poems, stories and photographs are spun together to explore deep interconnected themes of art, music, sex, drugs, drink, dependence, denial, self-destructiveness, and self-growth. Alago's book is original, moving, and very brave with insights beaming with beauty, sympathy, and compassion. Beautifully rendered, I can imagine this book saving somebody's life.

❊   ❊   ❊

John Joseph—Cro-Mags "JM" front man, author of *The PMA Effect.*

I've known Michael almost thirty-five years now and he remains one of my best friends. Michael is one of the most giving, sincere, humble humans I know, as he is always there in service for people who may be struggling with some of the issues, we all have, namely addiction. Throughout the years, through all the tests and adversity he has faced, his passion and love for music, the arts and especially people, is truly incredible. I've never told him this, but as an artist that's why I call him just about every single day. He inspires the fuck out of me, pushes me on to be creative in life, to stay determined, to always have that next project. Some may talk the talk . . . but Michael always walks the walk.

INTRODUCTION

The ritual of encounter is framed at the beginning and at the end with blessing. Regularly throughout conversation in Gaelic, there is explicit recognition that the divine is present in others. This presence is also recognized and embodied in old sayings such as, "the hand of the stranger is the hand of God." The stranger does not come accidentally; he brings a particular gift and illumination.[1]

Music has always been everything to me. It has gifted me with an amazing world filled with exceptional human beings I've had the honor and privilege to know, and with whom I've remained friends to this day.

To get there, I was taught by a remarkable woman—my mom, Blanche. She taught me how to be independent, self-reliant, and thoughtful. Through her guidance, I grew into someone who is not afraid to be truthful about who I am.

In 1980, entrepreneur and risk-taker Jerry Brandt hired me to assist him at The Ritz nightclub in New York City. He became my mentor, and not only did he teach me the art of the music business—he fueled my passion to be in it—and stay in it.

Three years later, in 1983, through the generous spirit of Bob Krasnow, chairman of Elektra Records, I was hired at the company, and not only was I able to become an important part of the music business and make major decisions—such as signing Metallica and re-introducing the legendary Nina Simone to the music world—Bob gave me room to grow and mature and become the kind of executive I knew I could be.

I also learned about the kind of person I wanted to be outside of music. That person has tried to be strong and authentic. In telling you this story about my life, I hope to show that it is okay to be truthful about who you are. I am gay and have been able to help extraordinary artists succeed; I have survived AIDS, and have been sober for twelve years. I have also published books of beautiful men that I have photographed and I passionately collect photography and art.

I knew from a very early age that I was gay, and it has defined my life in many marvelous ways. It has also brought surprising intolerance, which I have never let affect my life decisions. One of the first places I sensed this intolerance was in the world of heavy metal music, which was the focus of my work as a record executive.

Being gay in the world of heavy metal was never, ever heard of in the seventies and eighties. We loved Freddie Mercury of Queen, but he never came out of the closet. Only in recent years has Rob Halford, from Judas Priest, come out and, thank God, that hasn't hurt his career at all. "[I]sn't it great that in this day and age that we can think, '[Y]eah, we know Rob's gay. We love Judas Priest. Who gives a fuck?'"[2]

> The openly gay Alago represented a breath of fresh air on the sometimes casually homophobic world of metal. "My sexuality was never a problem with any artist I ever worked with," he explains. "When somebody is honest, truthful, and an open book, that helps. I was always myself. And that breaks down so many barriers. There's no need to talk about sexuality, when all we really want to talk about is music."[3]

Make no mistake though, the journey I have embarked on has been demanding and overwhelming. I have had to battle AIDS and serious drug and alcohol addiction. Thankfully, I survived those battles, am here to talk about it, and have come to a greater sense of peace and joy about my place in this world.

Many wonderful things have happened along the way, and many unfortunate things as well. Yet, in the end, that's the gift, isn't it? The more challenging the road traveled, the greater the reward.

As you will see.

> For me, prayer is an aspiration of the heart, it is a simple glance directed to heaven, it is a cry of gratitude and love in the midst of trial as well as joy; finally it is something great, supernatural, which expands my soul and unites me to Jesus.
>
> —St. Thérèse de Lisieux

1

BROOKLYN

I came out of the womb loving music. There was never a day that music didn't encompass my every waking moment. In 1966, I started listening to 77 WABC on my portable transistor radio—The Beatles, Steppenwolf, Aretha Franklin, Martha and the Vandellas, Mitch Ryder and the Detroit Wheels, The Beach Boys, and Dusty Springfield. A few years later, I watched Creedence Clearwater Revival, Gladys Knight and the Pips, Grand Funk Railroad, and Todd Rundgren on *American Bandstand*, *Don Kirshner's Rock Concert*, and *Soul Train*. That music was my lifeline, it was my nourishment—that was how I grew up, it was the beginning of my journey.

❁   ❁   ❁

I was raised in Brooklyn, New York. My mom, Blanche, a small-framed, petite beauty with dark, shining hair, worked as a Spanish-English interpreter. My dad, Anthony, who was in the Air Force and named "Airman of the Month" in 1955, ended up working for IBM. At the time my parents met, they were both working for District 65 on Astor Place in the East Village of Manhattan. District 65 was a labor union and catered to its members offering household goods for sale, eye glasses and a pharmacy—and happened to be where I ended up working years later.

My parents married in 1958. My mom was thirty-six years old, and my dad was twenty-five. They had me in October 1959, at Beth Israel Hospital in Manhattan and identified themselves as "white" on my birth certificate. Because the U.S. government didn't recognize Hispanics as a valid ethnic group until 1970, my parents had no place on the official hospital form to indicate they were Puerto Rican, so they just labeled themselves as "white."

From the moment I was born, my mom dressed me in three-piece suits and made sure I looked like a proper young man. It didn't matter where I went or what I did, I was always suited up.

Four years after I was born, my sister Cheryl arrived. It made my parents really happy, and I thought she was super cute. I remember holding her a lot, and even at that early age, we were inseparable. Every Christmas we always got tons of toys and stuffed animals. My favorites were Cecil and Beany, a plush green dinosaur and a little boy from the famous *Beany and Cecil* TV show. I also got G. I. Joes, Hasbro's Sno Cone Machine and Rock 'em Sock 'em Robots, while Cheryl got the doll Chatty Cathy and an Easy Bake Oven. We constantly played the games Operation and Candy Land on our gray, paisley couch, which was always covered in plastic by my mother because she kept an immaculate home. "My house is so clean, you could eat off the floor," she always said.

✻   ✻   ✻

We first lived in a small second floor apartment in a brownstone on Chauncey street in the Bushwick section of Brooklyn. Chauncey was famed for being the street where Lena Horne grew up as well as Jackie Gleason. In fact, Chauncey was the setting for *The Honeymooners* TV show in the fifties. That always made me chuckle because it kind of foretold my future of unexplained ties with celebrities, out of nowhere, like it was somehow meant to be.

When I was six years old, we moved to De Sales Place in East New York. The street was a cultural mix of Latino, Irish, Black, and Italian families. Because De Sales was a dead-end street and we were always out on the stoops talking, playing and hanging around—it often felt like one big family.

Whenever there was a huge snowstorm, everyone would get together and build a big hill of snow at the end of the street and we'd all go sledding down the makeshift white mountain. It was a unique and loving time for me, enhanced by all of the different ethnic groups and traditions living there.

I think the first tragedy I ever heard or knew of in my life was when little Albert Robinson, one of the kids in the black family, was hit by a car and dragged for blocks and blocks and died. It was the first time I ever saw anything so disturbing. It shook the entire neighborhood.

❆ ❆ ❆

I didn't come from a musical family and I didn't come from a small family. I came from a big, busy Latino family that had roots in Puerto Rico and Cuba, and the most important rule drummed into us from day one was: *"You don't ask people for help, you don't tell people your business, you do for yourself and never, ever talk about anything that happened in the family. Period."*

Whatever occurred—as far as my mother was concerned—you did not discuss. Silence wasn't just the golden rule, it was law. That, as you will see, became a very tricky problem for me.

My mom had three sisters and one brother—Ursula, Barbara, Aida, and Mike. Aida was my Mom's identical twin sister and she adored me. She always insisted I was *"her"* Michael." She lived on West 76th Street in Manhattan, and although Titi Aida had two children—Connie and Joseph—they weren't raised by her. In fact, we were told Joseph died at birth, and we only learned much later that he was alive and had been given up for adoption.

It was like that with the rest of my mom's family, as well—she and my aunts and uncles weren't raised by their parents, but their grandparents.

However, there was a great deal of loyalty, and that devotion spread to all of us. At the same time, the world inside the family was very controlled. It wasn't ever discussed that Titi Aida's son was alive and living somewhere else, and it was never brought up that—she may have been gay.

One day after a visit with Titi Aida uptown, as were walking to the IRT train to go home, I asked Mom where Titi Aida's friend, Mary, slept. Mary was there every time we visited. It seemed to me she was obviously living with her, plus there was only one bedroom. The moment I asked, my mom promptly slapped me across the head, and we continued walking home in silence. There was to be no talking about that situation, or *any* situation—*ever*.

Titi Aida wasn't just my Titi, she was also a practitioner of "Santeria." Santeria is an Afro-American religion from the Caribbean which is influenced by the Roman Catholic Church. Titi Aida believed she was an "Oricha," which is similar to a priestess or a guide—within the spiritual world of Santeria.

When I was very young, maybe a preteen, and there was a big family get-together, everyone usually congregated at my great Titi Mary's house in Borough Park. We all sat around her huge oak wood dining room table and there were always loud conversations going on as we ate yellow rice, red beans, and platanos.

Titi Mary lived in a railroad apartment and, often at some point in the evening, Titi Aida would disappear into the living room. At first, I wasn't sure what was happening, but I soon learned she was going to pray and it usually ended up with her going into a trance—almost like a convulsion. It always scared me, but my mom would guide me into the room and say, "Go on, she's here to bless you."

Titi Aida usually sat in a big chair and smoked a cigar while she was in the trance. She rocked back and forth and took my hands, putting them on top of each other, then tapping them together. She would then start wiping me down—cleansing me, in a very spiritual way. It was like a renewal. She did all this while blowing cigar smoke everywhere and saying her blessings in both Spanish and English. She seemed very, very far away—except she was right there in front of us.

I think mom was right, because last year when I was in Cuba with my friend Lionel, we took a motorboat to an island off the port of Havana called Regla, where we met a Santeria priestess. She asked me if I would like a blessing. I nodded.

"Oh, there's somebody here with us," the priestess said to me. "I can't tell if they've passed or if they're still here on earth—but they practice Santeria."

"Oh, that's my Titi Aida!"

She laughed. "Ah, yes!" she exclaimed. "She's here! Recognize that she's here." Then she raised her arms into the air and shouted:

"Your Titi Aida says to tell you she loves you so VERY much!"

The strange thing is, that was the exact same way my Titi Aida ended every conversation with me, raising her voice into the phone in that exaggerated manner, declaring she loved me. I was sure she was there in Cuba with me.

❁   ❁   ❁

My Dad had two sisters, Jennie and Irma. They all lived together in a brownstone in East New York, with his parents and grandmother. Everybody had their own unique personalities. Titi Irma was really strict and kept her door closed all the time, so I didn't see much of my cousins, Lisa and Kim.

My Titi Jennie, whose children, Johnny and Julie, lived there as well—was very cool, and I spent a lot of time with her. She listened to the music of artists like Isaac Hayes, Nancy Wilson, Johnny Mathis, and Nina Simone. She also was gorgeous. There was a vibe about her that I connected to from a very early age. My dad's family was very close, but the dynamic was strange.

When we moved to De Sales Place, I started first grade at Our Lady of Lourdes Catholic School. It was only one and a half blocks from our house, so I was allowed to walk there by myself. It was a co-ed school, but the boys and girls were kept separate all the time. I had two best friends—Stanley Curry and Jimmy Lovett. Stanley always came home with me after school to have cream cheese and jelly sandwiches on white bread, which my mom made for us. Jimmy lived just a few doors down from my house. He came from a big Irish family—maybe eight or nine kids.

Sometimes, after school, we played Skully on the street with a bunch of the other neighborhood kids. We took some chalk and drew specially numbered boxes in a square board on the street. There were twelve boxes along the edge and in the middle was the thirteenth box—the "Skully" box. We flicked bottle caps across the board on the pavement, trying to get them into each of the boxes but not in the Skully box or we'd lose. The one whose cap was the last survivor on the board, won. To help us win, we often melted wax and plopped it into one of the bottle caps to give it weight for easier gliding across the cement. If one of us was really slick—we took the cap off the soda bottle, rubbed the glass top against the concrete until it came off, and smoothed it out into a beautiful glass ring.

✻   ✻   ✻

When I was twelve years old my parents separated, and, a year later, they divorced. I'm not entirely sure what happened, but I know my mother threw my dad out when she caught him cheating on her.

Although only four feet ten inches tall, my mother towered over all of us. She was a very determined lady and had a strong spirit, which came from her deep and devoted commitment to religion. It may have been that devotion that contributed to my parents' problems. I do know my dad was nowhere near as religious as Mom, and he rarely went to church with us.

If you ask me, I think my mom only had sex twice in her life—to conceive my sister and me. I also think as a result of that, my dad became a bit of a womanizer. I'm sure that created tension. I remember my mother crying a lot after the separation and talking on the phone to her best girl-friend, Ada, who lived in the Bronx. I'm not sure how my dad felt, though he visited us a lot—a couple times a week in the beginning. Later, we only saw him on Saturdays.

My mother took us to church every Sunday. I was captivated by the service and the rituals—I loved the incense smells and the communion ceremony. I loved the formality and the idea of prayer. It was the mid-sixties, and we still prayed and said the Pledge of Allegiance in school and it gave me a great sense of safety.

Every single day of my mom's life, she lit a candle to St. Jude to protect and guide Cheryl and me. St. Jude was one of the twelve apostles, and he was known for his compassion for the sick and dying, his ability to work wonders, to cure the incurable, and make people whole again. Mom was entirely dedicated to him and, without fail, she regularly lit a candle to him until the day she died. I am convinced that this devotion protected and saved me through the unimaginable risks I took during my adult life—and still does.

After the divorce was final, we moved to New Utrecht Avenue and I enrolled in St. Frances de Chantal for sixth grade. It was closer to my Titi Mary's home, because my mom wanted us to be near her.

During this time, Mom was still working as an English-Spanish Interpreter, so every day after school Cheryl and I went to Titi Mary's house until Mom got home from work. She lived near us on 54th Street in Borough Park, where she took care of her mother, my great Abuela Ursula.

Titi Mary was a saint. She had gone through a divorce some years previously and taken in Abuela Ursula, watching over her until her dying day.

Titi Mary was also very posh. She had fancy furniture made by Haywood-Wakefield around the house and made sure all of us lounged in the lap of luxury when we visited. She also kept her look impeccable for her entire life—even her gray hair was pristine. She used Alberto VO5 hair conditioner, and it shined with more brilliance than the mirrors in her hallway. I can *still* smell the VO5 she had on every day.

Abuela Ursula was quite a character, and I adored her. When I went over to Titi Mary's after school, Abuela would be working on her thousand-piece jigsaw puzzle at the end of the dining room table. She didn't speak any English and I spoke only a little Spanish—essentially, Spanglish—but I understood her, she made perfect sense to me.

She had trouble with her legs, so she usually sat at the table or in her rocking chair, and I would tease her to climb onto her lap. I nudged her and nudged her. Then she would let out a big sigh and scream in Spanish:

"*¡Deja de ser un chico malo!*" while banging her cane on the floor. I laughed so loud at her, then I would give her a big kiss.

She had this little blue-starred handkerchief with which she tied up her money and kept in her pocket. Very often she would show it to me.

"*¡Tu madre y tu hermana me roban!*" she said, winking, as she gestured with her hand, signaling her handkerchief being taken from her. I just shook my head and said:

"Abuela! Mommy and Cheryl didn't rob you!"

But she would lift her head, arch her nose into the air, and say, with absolute certainty: "*Hm!*"

She knew I was right, but she wouldn't give in. When I was there, I also watched afternoon TV with her and Titi Mary. Whenever they turned it to Channel 7 to watch *One Life to Live*, Cheryl and I crawled under the dining room table and laid there with our chins on our fists. It was so much fun, particularly when we watched *Dark Shadows*, which we adored. We got really excited when we saw the characters Barnabas and Quentin Collins. I was so crazy for Quentin that I took the first name of the actor, David Selby, who played him, as my confirmation name.

We also lived in a large Hasidic neighborhood. We were the only Puerto Rican family in the building, so on Saturdays, during the Sabbath, the Hasidim would open their door slightly and ask me to come into their apartment and turn off their lights because it was prohibited by Torah law for them to touch the switches. I carefully went in and turned off each light, and every time I did, they paid me a quarter or fifty cents.

Our home was a railroad apartment right in front of the elevated B subway train. My dad went back to live with his family, and we continued to see him on Saturdays. I just loved those visits with him. We would watch women's roller derby and play the "License Plate" game in the car. Cheryl usually sat in the front and I sat in the back with my head hung between the two front seats, so I wouldn't miss anything. We would look furiously around the streets while my dad drove, trying to be the first to shout when we saw an out-of-state license plate. At some point, we drove back to De Sales place where he was living and spent the rest of the day going through everybody's apartment—my grandparents, my Titi Jennie, sometimes my Titi Irma—and my great grandmother Abuela Carmen, who was very old and also never learned English. She was always making stuff. She carried a hammer and nails in the pocket of her housecoat and had tons of images of saints in her apartment.

My dad eventually had a few girlfriends, which made me very unhappy. One of his girlfriends had a son, whom she brought to the house one day. The kid sat on the sofa next to Cheryl and me. I promptly pushed him off. He didn't belong there, and I made sure he knew it.

In October 1978, my dad got remarried. Her name was Gloria and they had a son named, Matthew—my brother. Gloria turned out to be a wonderful woman for my dad and us. I'm very proud of Matt, who went to work for CBS Sports and ended up winning an Emmy in 2011, for Outstanding New Approaches in Sports Programming for the web series *A Game of Honor*. I'm so grateful for the love and warmth that Gloria and Matthew have brought into my life.

2

VULNERABLE

I was a bit of a loner. I often sat on the stoop of our building in Borough Park, listening to 7-inch 45 records on my gray, portable Panasonic record player. I also listened to AM radio, which, in the early seventies, wasn't heavily formatted at all. It was very organic and ranged from pop to hard rock to R&B. I would hear Rare Earth's "I Just Wanna Celebrate" and right after that Aretha singing "Respect," then Grand Funk Railroad's "I'm Your Captain/Closer to Home." Between WABC and my Panasonic, that's all I needed. At other times, I would stay in my room with the door shut, dancing and dreaming. I didn't care about people or anything, I just cared about listening to music—it was heaven.

I attended St. Frances de Chantal until I graduated to high school. One of my favorite early memories was walking home from school in seventh grade and hearing music coming out of an old store front where the windows had been covered up with sheets. I peeked past the edge of one of the sheets and saw three long-haired musicians banging out this amazing music—very Led Zeppelin-like. It was mesmerizing. Every afternoon, I walked by there, sat outside and listened, completely captivated.

I learned later the band was called Sir Lord Baltimore and they had an album out on Mercury Records called *Kingdom Come*. One of the older neighborhood kids had the album and showed it to me. It was the first "gatefold" album cover I ever saw, and I was in awe. Along with the music, the thing that captured me was the artwork. Art and photography would become worlds I obsessively traveled in as much as rock 'n' roll. I also learned later that Sir Lord Baltimore's style was considered very new, very different from traditional rock at the time, and was described in *Creem* magazine as "heavy metal"[1]—one of the first times that phrase was ever used.

Around that same time period, we got *TV Guide* every week. In the center was an advertisement for Columbia House Records, and you could order ten records for a penny. But of course, being young and clueless, we never read the fine print. If we had, we would have seen that every record after that was $4.99, which, to a young pre-teen, was a lot of money! What I remember specifically about signing on with Columbia House was ordering Alice Cooper's *Killer* album. I knew about him because I saw him on *Don Kirshner's Rock Concert*, and I was completely enthralled by his theatricality.

✻   ✻   ✻

As I knew from a very young age about my passion for music, I also knew that I liked men. I fooled around with the neighborhood boys a lot and although we know that young kids experiment, I liked it a lot more than the rest of them. The thing was, even if I didn't have the word for homosexual or gay, I was attracted to them. We would go behind a wall at the cemetery, or in somebody's home basement and pull down our pants and show each other what we had—I just loved it. It was a precursor to my later life, and my adoration of men.

However, I actually had a girlfriend for one minute. Her name was Tammy and I lost my virginity to her. She lived around the corner by New Utrecht Avenue on 55th Street, with her mom, Gina, and her younger sister, Kim. Gina was very "gangsta." She worked at a bar in Manhattan and was very close with Jilly Rizzo, whose saloon, on West 49th Street, was a popular celebrity hangout. Rizzo was also Frank Sinatra's best friend. Gina kept herself very put together, with long shiny fingernails and a well-done frosted blonde shag haircut. Whenever she went to work, Tammy and I fooled around. But that was it for me and girls.

As for my homosexuality, I never knew about that phrase "being in the closet." So I guess I was "out" since the day I was born. I never hid it. When I was fourteen or so, I even went so far as wearing crushed velvet purple shorts around the neighborhood. I remember thinking to myself, "Oh, honey, this is a little outrageous!" but all I wondered was how do I add to the flamboyance, not how to tone it down.

In fact, at 86th Street and New Utrecht Avenue, which was in the heart of Bensonhurst, there was a very "hip" shopping area with a store called The Farm. It sold fringe jackets and elephant bell bottom jeans. They also had these beige high-heeled wedge sandals for women that I bought for myself, and happily paraded around the neighborhood wearing them. I had zero fear of what people would say about me. I don't know where that came from so, in a peculiar way, I never saw a closet.

❋   ❋   ❋

In May 1973, my dad's mother, Marie, died. She was the matriarch of the family and her death shook everyone. My dad was devastated. He had been very close with her—a mama's boy from a very early age. He was inconsolable.

My grandfather was also grief-stricken, and that was an unexpected sight for me. He was an army man from WWII, and had a very stern and stoic way about him. But when my grandmother died, I saw something in him change. It was like a part of him physically died with her. His body language altered—he started to slump and drag himself everywhere.

I remember being at the house a lot with the family, for support, and one time, my grandfather asked me to come to his apartment by myself. He was feeling very depressed, and when I got there, things turned strange. He asked me to come to his bedroom and had me lie down on the bed. I didn't understand what he was doing so I just followed orders. Suddenly, he climbed on top of me. He was fully clothed and after some time passed, he satisfied himself. I was stunned. I was thirteen years old and I didn't know what to think.

The confusing thing was that afterwards, I went back to his apartment a few more times. I still don't know why. He died two years later.

That experience with my grandfather, that molesting, that groping—not only left me shaken but it threw me into a place of complete self-protection, which exists to this day. It ruined my ability to be open and vulnerable to getting involved with a man in an intimate relationship. It set me up to prevent that kind of abuse from ever happening again. I began spending more and more time alone, which, in an odd way, I preferred.

Yet, something inside me, I don't know what, moved me to find a professional to talk to—a doctor, a therapist, a counselor—even though not discussing anything of importance was set into my bones from a very early age. I sensed that what had happened to me was wrong, and that it might cause me a lot of problems in the future.

I came across a "teen clinic" at Maimonides Hospital in Borough Park. That's where I met Danny Papa, a community mental health worker. I started meeting with him once a week and we discussed many issues concerning my mental health, but only as much as my fourteen-year old brain could handle, so of course, I never told him about my grandfather's abuse.

In later years, I realized that if I had told him about the assault, he would have contacted the medical team at Maimonides because it was required by law that he report any physical or mental abuse communicated by a client. But he never had to call them for me, because I never said anything.

At some point, Danny gained my trust, and I felt he had taken a liking to me. We started talking about our mutual interest in music and photography and he asked me many questions about what I wanted to do in my life.

Our relationship became more than counselor and client. After some time, Danny invited me to his home to meet his wife, Maria, and we ended up spending a lot of time together as they took a very kind interest in me. I spent many evenings there, playing backgammon and watching

TV as we got to know each other better. It became a safe haven for me. I think Danny was concerned that my father wasn't around much and, although I was close with my mother, I believe he felt there was something missing for me. Danny and Maria soon became a second family for me, and I have been blessed to know them, their daughters Jennifer and Corrin, as well as their grandchildren—to this day. It is a relationship I treasure with all my heart and soul.

3

MUSIC. ART. THEATRE.

One day, we visited my mom's sister, Titi Bobbie. She lived in the Barri Projects on Staten Island. Heavyset and strikingly beautiful, Titi Bobbie was a scream and I loved visiting her and my cousins Carole Ann and Louis. Louis was an athlete, and Carole Ann—stunning like her mother—loved music. She was also dating a guy from Queens whom I called, "Manny the Greek from Astoria."

On this particular visit, Manny was talking about tickets he had to go see Alice Cooper's "Billion Dollar Babies" Tour, at Madison Square Garden. He was trying to get Carole Ann to go with him, but she was feeling sick from her period and just wanted to stay home and listen to Marvin Gaye.

"Take my little cousin,' she said to Manny. "He'll want to go."

I looked up at Manny the Greek and smiled harder than I ever had before.

The next week, I went to meet him at his job at Lord &Taylor on Fifth Avenue in Manhattan. We planned go to the Alice Cooper concert that evening, when his shift ended. He worked on the second floor in the men's department and I was completely taken by the place. I remember when I first walked in, I was afraid to touch anything—cashmere sweaters, double-breasted suits, bottles of Fabergé men's cologne. I had never before seen *any* place so fancy and upscale. We weren't there very long, though, because Manny punched out a few minutes after I arrived, and we grabbed the subway to the show.

It was my first time at Madison Square Garden, and it was a real eye-opener. All the fans pouring into the venue looked glamorous in their pink and purple costumes and their striped top-hats and tails.

We made our way to our seats. The lights dimmed and suddenly a large white spotlight appeared and Alice emerged on stage. I was riveted. He had on a top hat and white leotards with leopard platform boots stretching up over his knees. On his face were spider eyes created with theatrical black greasepaint and mascara. He had a cane which he twirled around like a wand, pointing it at the audience as if he was about to flash something wondrous and magical at us. The stage production totally blew me away. The music was loud and hard. Alice and the band opened up the with "Hello, Hooray" and ripped through "School's Out," "I'm Eighteen," and "No More Mr. Nice Guy," then they encored with "Under My Wheels." The show was incredible.

That was June 3, 1973, the last night of the "Billion Dollar Babies" tour in NYC, and my first rock concert. It changed my life forever. I already had the *Killer* album, but I didn't have the previous records, *Pretties for you*, *Easy Action*, or *Love it to Death*. So, one day, I took the subway over to E. J. Korvettes on Bay Parkway, to get them all. I also started buying all the popular music publications like *Circus*, *Rock Scene*, *Creem*, and *Rolling Stone*.

During this same time, I had been visiting my dad in Manhattan on Saturdays. He worked for IBM on Astor Place. I spent those days futzing around the office, but one of the best things about the Saturday visits was the magazine stand right around the corner. That's where I discovered *The Village Voice* and *After Dark Magazine*.

After Dark catered to up-and-coming artists, musicians, dancers, and actors. It featured the upscale photography of Martha Swope and Jack Mitchell. On the glossy pages there were beautiful, half-naked men, which is part of the reason I obsessively bought it.

But my new bible was *The Village Voice*. I dug through every single page of that newspaper. It listed everything that was happening in New York City: shows like Todd Rundgren's *Utopia Tour* at Radio City Music Hall to Patti Smith at CBGB's and the latest porn stars performing at XXX-male burlesque theaters in Times Square. I found everything I had always wanted: concerts, Broadway, movies, porn. Actually, I found myself.

❊   ❊   ❊

I started ninth grade at an all-boys Catholic high school called Bishop Ford. During my first two years, I kept up my school work and attendance like my mom wanted, but effectively, I was leaving Brooklyn—a lot.

In 1974, I went to the Felt Forum to see Lou Reed. That same year, I saw an R&B revue there featuring the Spinners, Ashford & Simpson, and Graham Central Station. I also saw Aerosmith and David Bowie's *Diamond Dogs Tour* at the Garden. I was driven, I was fixated on seeing everything—absorbing music, art, concerts, theatre—everything.

One day I decided to go see LaBelle at The Apollo Theatre in Harlem, and I didn't tell my mother. In fact, I cut school to do it. It was not unusual for me to get home late, even on school nights. My mom and I had an understanding that getting home late was fine, as long as I kept up my grades—which I did. But I had never cut school before.

Patti LaBelle was gorgeous and gave a show-stopping performance at the Apollo—even at eight months pregnant. She worked that stage in the most electrifying way. Whenever I went to a concert, I never, ever stayed in my seat and it was no different at the Labelle show. I ran up to the front of the stage and danced out of control. I wanted to be as close to her as humanly possible.

Around midnight when the concert was over, I was heading back to Brooklyn on the B train and as we got closer to my stop, I suddenly saw my mother through the train window. She was standing in the doorway of our building in her housecoat, armed with a broom. I started getting nervous.

I was trembling as I stepped down the stairs to the sidewalk. Within moments, she furiously shook the broom at me.

"Where were you?" she screamed.

"I went to a concert—" I said.

"Where did you go to a concert?" she demanded.

I didn't want to tell her it was all the way up in Harlem, so I told her I was at Madison Square Garden, where I'd seen Alice Cooper with Manny.

"And, by the way," she snapped, as she tightened her grip on the broom. "How was school today?"

"Good," I replied, trying to get past her to the stairs.

"You didn't go to school today!" she screamed, raising the broom to my face.

Apparently, the principal at Bishop Ford had called her that day asking if I was sick because I hadn't shown up.

Mom grounded me for two weeks and I vowed to never cut school again, or, if I did, to make sure she never found out about it.

※   ※   ※

The following year, 1975, I went to as many Broadway shows as I could. I saw Bette Midler in her *Clams on the Half Shell Revue* at The Minskoff Theatre. She performed with the Lionel Hampton Orchestra and I sat in the front row, although I have no idea how I got front-row tickets. I brought my Panasonic cassette recorder with me, which I hid in my green knapsack. Then once the lights went down, I carefully pulled the recorder out and taped the whole show. Afterwards, I headed to the backstage door to meet her and get her autograph. I went to see her show about five or six more times.

I also went to the Broadway debut of *The Rocky Horror Show* at The Belasco Theater. Although the show didn't do too well—it closed after forty-seven performances—I loved it. After the many times I went to the show, I was determined to get backstage to meet Tim Curry. With my friends Sunny Bak and Frank Tedi—both young paparazzi—I wondered how, as we waited by the stage door, do we maneuver ourselves in to meet Curry and take his picture? Sunny was a little startled at my plan.

"We can't go backstage!" she said.

"Of course, we can!" I said with complete confidence. "We're going backstage!"

When we finally got in, we saw Tim Curry heading out with a very young Meatloaf behind him. I approached them and told them how fantastic I thought they were and asked them to take a picture with me. I ended up seeing *Rocky Horror* at least a dozen more times. I also wound up "second-acting" it, which involved waiting for everyone to come outside during intermission for a smoke, then casually walking back in for the performance and grabbing any empty seat I could find.

I think I got that *chutzpah* from my mom, although I don't know if she would agree. She always drummed that family credo into us: "You do for yourself!" and that fueled my independence.

I then went to the opening night of *A Chorus Line*. I had a $10 balcony seat which was just so awful that when the lights went down, I quickly looked around, and seeing an empty seat on the orchestra floor, ran to it and quietly climbed in. At intermission, when the lights went up, I turned my head and saw the famed underground actor Divine sitting in the next seat. It was astounding. I knew who he was from the John Waters films, but I couldn't believe I was sitting next to him and he was all dolled up. Curiously, Divine would end up popping up at surprising moments in my life. I was so enchanted by his appearance, all I could do was stare at him that evening, and the odd thing was that I didn't say anything—which wasn't like me at all.

✿   ✿   ✿

In the fall, I started at City-As-School. I was in eleventh grade and I'd had enough of Catholic schools. I had been attending them for ten years and I told my mom that I needed to do something different. It's not that I felt Catholic school was bad, I was just really tired of it. It was very restrictive, and I wanted more freedom. It wasn't that I planned to cut classes a lot or ditch school completely. I just needed more open-mindedness from my teachers and fellow students. Attending City-As-School also helped me in my quest to get out of Brooklyn and into Manhattan.

City-As-School was experimental, and classes weren't held in a stuffy room inside a big, cement building. We were farmed out all over the city to work in internships and learn in more creative and imaginative ways—an approach that attracted innovative, artistic types of kids. Jean Michel Basquiat was one of those kids and we often had a class together at 100 Livingston Street in Brooklyn. We hung out on the front steps and he always had a black & white composition book with him in which he constantly doodled. He often showed me his amazing illustrations—they were abstract, childlike, very primitive. They looked like hieroglyphics—and they spoke to me. In fact, I remember seeing one of his best-known paintings—*Famous Negro Athletes*—in a very early form in one of those books. He would say to me, as he fanatically drew, "I'm gonna become famous!"

And he did. In fact, a number of years later, I visited him at 57 Great Jones Street in Manhattan. Andy Warhol had purchased that building for him to live and work in because he was completely under Warhol's wing by then. Basquiat was having a Christmas party and even though we were off doing our own things at that point, we spotted each other on the street one day and he invited me to his holiday party.

When I rang the doorbell, and the door opened, wafts of pot smoke poured out, and Francesco Clemente was standing there. I gulped, trying not to gawk at him, and introduced myself, then maneuvered through the smoking, swaying crowd, all the way to the back. I found Jean Michel feverishly painting on a canvas. He was definitely high, and he instantly recognized me. It was clear he had been stoned for a while—his eyes were glazed, and his skin was ravaged from the constant picking that junkies tend to do. He then offered me one of his composition books, in memory of our many days sitting on the front stoop at school. But I said no. When someone is so out of their mind like he was at that moment, I just couldn't accept his offer. Unfortunately, he was dead from an overdose only a few years later.

4

PATTI

In art and dream may you proceed with abandon.
In life may you proceed with balance and stealth.[1]

The first time I ever saw Patti Smith was in 1974. She was doing a poetry reading in celebration of the French poet Arthur Rimbaud. She inspired my heart and soul. In December of 1975, her debut album, *Horses*, was released, and just like what happened when I saw Alice Cooper, my life went through a radical shift.

It was as if Patti was from another planet—that whole androgynous look of hers in the now-classic photo by Robert Mapplethorpe—there was a true Frank Sinatra swagger to it—very cool and confident.

Right after I got the album and devoured it, I was obsessed with her. She was a true visionary in her music, art, and poetry.

charms. sweet angels—you have made me no longer afraid of death.[2]

After *Horses* came out, I felt an intense need to get hold of everything I could about her. I picked up the phone and called the Wartoke Concern— the company listed as her publicity agent on the back of the album. When her publicist, Jeffi Powell, answered, I said: "Hi, I'm Michael Alago, I live in Brooklyn. I'm a big fan of Patti's and I bought the *Horses* album. Is there any kind of press kit that I could get?"

She was pretty abrupt with me. I actually could hear her sighing. I'm sure she was rolling her eyes too. It sounded like she had been fielding a lot of media and my phone call just added to her nerve-racking day. Who was I really? Not the press, not a concert promoter, but she said she would send me something soon.

Well, I waited, and I waited, and I waited, and after about two months, a big packet of press info arrived, and it was a real shock—it had everything I could have ever wanted about Patti in it. On top of that, Ms. Powell sent me a letter with the packet, apologizing for the delay. I was amazed, and in hindsight, I realized that was a real stretch for her—I was just another teenage fan.

I went to see Patti a few months later with my friend Lori Reese. Lori worked at Outrageous Records in Brooklyn and we had met at City-As-School. We were both rabid Patti fans, and in July of 1976, we got tickets for her show at the Central Park Schaefer Music Festival. We were dancing and screaming, pumping our fists in the air. Patti was exactly what we wanted and needed. After the show, Lori and I walked to the backstage area to see if we could catch a glimpse of her and the band leaving the venue.

In fact, as they were walking out, we got that chance and were able to say "Hi" to Patti and Lenny Kaye and Richard Sohl. I also took a picture of Lori and Patti with my Kodak instamatic 110. We were both so overwhelmed by her. Since then, I have had a number of profound moments with Patti, and we also became close at a very painful point later in my life.

In the eighties, Patti retired from performing to move to St. Claire Shores, Michigan, to live with her husband, Fred "Sonic" Smith from MC5, and raise their two children, Jessie and Jackson. But beginning in 1989, with the passing of her closest friend, Robert Mapplethorpe, death began to surround her. Five years later, her husband died of a heart attack and a few weeks after that, her brother Todd died from a fatal stroke. Around that same time, I was suffering from full-blown AIDS and I received many loving phone calls from Patti. She knew I had been her devoted fan for the previous twenty years, and I can only assume the compassionate spirit and kindness which generated this series of phone calls to me came as a result of the overwhelming losses she had recently been going through.

Phone Call March 1994

Patti: Well, you sound great Michael.

Me: Well, you know, Patti—I thank God I'm feeling good right now.

Patti: 'Cause I've talked to you when you sounded very different, and you sound really good.

Me: Well, my stomach is back in order, I really don't even know that anything is the matter.

Patti: Robert always said if he could get his stomach together, he could handle anything.

Me: Right!

Patti: And that's what got Fred—his stomach was worse than his heart—his stomach, and he had bad nerves his whole life. You don't think much about the dark stomach until you need it!

Me: Yup. yup. You know, when the stomach starts to go it just triggers everything else, and you wind up having to run to the bathroom and becoming dehydrated—oh, its hideous!

Patti: Well, stay up there, Michael.

Me: I'm tryin', girl!

Patti: You're doin' great! You've been working. I think that's great. I think you really—you're an inspiration to people, you keep going . . .

Me: Thank you.

Patti: I hope everything works out.

Me: Me, too. So Friday, Washington Square Hotel?

Patti: We'll go to the library together.

Me: That'd be fun, fabulous. Oh, it's so nice to hear your voice!

Patti: You, too!

Me: Bye.

Patti: Bye.[3]

During one of those many phone calls, Patti also read "The Day of My Death" by Pasolini, from his book *Roman Poems*.

> In a city, Trieste or Udine,
> along the linden boulevard,
> when in spring
> the leaves change color,
> I'll drop dead
> under the ardent sun,
> blond and tall,
> and I'll close my eyes,
> leaving the sky to its splendor.
> Under a warm green linden
> I'll fall into my death's darkness,
> scattering linden and sun.
> The beautiful boys
> will run in that light
> which I've just lost,
> flying from school
> with curls on their brows. [4]

Later, she told me how excited she was about going into the studio to record a few demos. She played me her voice-and-piano versions of "Don't Smoke in Bed" by Nina Simone and "When the Hunter Gets Captured by the Game" by the Marvelettes. A few days later, she mailed me a cassette of the songs. Needless to say, I was over the moon.

In early 1995, Patti sent me a draft of her book on Robert Mapplethorpe entitled *The Coral Sea*. Her editor, Amy Cherry of Norton Publishing,
asked me not to circulate it because they weren't planning on publishing it
until the following year. It covered Robert's life as a young man, his relationship with Sam Wagstaff, his professional accomplishments, and his struggle
and death from AIDS.

> And the eye became a body, the murky heart of a rose. The sinister shadow
> of an orchid. Or the indolent poppy balanced behind the ear of Baudelaire. [5]

The Coral Sea references Robert's photos, which are elegantly displayed
throughout the book. To my shock and deep appreciation, Patti acknowledged six people at the end of *The Coral Sea*, including myself.

> In my opinion, Patti Smith is the smartest and most charismatic artist
> living today.

—Michael Alago

5

A NEW FAMILY

The moment I became a teenager, I already knew there was a world outside that I planned to explore. My mind detached from everything Brooklyn, and everything family. In some strange way, my mom understood that. She knew that my passion was music, and she allowed me to go out at all hours, dress wildly, and hang with people unknown to her or to Brooklyn. I don't know if she knew I was gay—I had never brought it up as we never discussed anything meaningful or with any serious weight to it. But she must've known—a mother's instinct, I think. However, it was still bizarre how she let me wander out and over the East River into Manhattan because in the mid-seventies, the city was a very dangerous place for everyone, particularly a cute, pint-sized fourteen-year-old kid.

❊   ❊   ❊

Ultimately, I found an extended family in rock 'n' roll. The first place I descended upon was Max's Kansas City. Peter Crowley was Max's booking agent.

Peter's office was on the third floor and it was also where the dressing rooms were located. Since there was no official backstage, and the bands played on the second floor, the musicians and their friends were always running back and forth, up and down the stairs between the dressing rooms and the stage. As a result, I was always on the third floor—and that's when Peter and I became good friends.

Some of the first bands I saw at Max's were the Mumps, Cherry Vanilla, B-52s, Pylon, The Fast, New York Dolls, Wayne County and the Backstreet Boys, and my absolute favorite—Suicide.

Suicide was unique and complicated. It was synthesized, distorted, atmospheric and, early on, a sound I completely related to—I loved that kind of noise. When I heard it, I had a visceral reaction to it. It was very New York, dirty, gritty and in your face and it all came out of the synthesizers of Martin Rev. Alan Vega was the front man and singer—a true visionary. He sometimes beat himself with a mic and there'd be blood everywhere. He loved the theatre of it all. Alan and Martin told stories in their synthesized pieces about underground New York, addiction, criminals—even love. For me, there was a sense of spirituality throughout their music. Their first two albums are easily in the top ten records I cherish.

> . . . although it was Rev who came up with the minimalist keyboard riffs that would define Suicide's sound, much of the original sonic and visual template for the band was Vega's . . . Vega straddled the Warhol-dominated art world and the glam rock scene of early seventies . . . [he] roamed the stage like a feral Elvis, muttering and howling over Rev's Farfisa organ. . . .Famously, Suicide were the first band to actively describe their music as "'punk,'" and were equally famously reviled by fans of the later punk bands they opened for, such as The Clash and Siouxsie & The Banshees.[1]

Their song "Dream Baby Dream" was covered by Bruce Springsteen in 2014 and Bruce spoke very admirably about Alan Vega when he died in 2016:

> The bravery and passion he showed throughout his career was deeply influential to me. I was lucky enough to get to know Alan slightly and he was always a generous and sweet spirit. The blunt force power of his greatest music both

with Suicide and on his solo records can still shock and inspire today. There was simply no one else remotely like him.[2]

In reality, Alan's onstage, very dark performances usually cleared the room, and without fail, two or three fans, myself included, were the only ones left behind. I would sit still on those two little steps on the side of the Max's stage, worshipping him, the performance, and the noise. After the set was over, I invariably followed him upstairs to the third-floor dressing room and raved about how incredible I thought he was. I gushed, which Alan recalled years later, seemed so strange to him. But I loved him. He was a genius, a great artist—a painter, a sculptor—and I am so grateful that we became friends and stayed close until he passed away at the age of seventy-eight.

I also became close with Paul Zone of The Fast and, through Paul, Debbie Harry of Blondie. Debbie and Paul were good friends and they were around Max's all the time. In fact, Paul's band, The Fast, was practically the house band there as he was also the DJ. His two brothers, Mandy and Miki, made up the rest of the band. They were glam/pop and very sought-after on the scene. Mandy was a big, lovable, hairy teddy bear and he and I hit it off like a house on fire. Every time we saw each other we wound up hootin' and hollerin', and laughing so hard our stomachs hurt. I was sure the entire neighborhood could hear us, and it was always a blast.

✵   ✵   ✵

I became a regular at Max's. I was either in Peter's office, or hanging backstage with the musicians after their sets were over.

Whenever I arrived, the front door was usually manned by Tommy Dean, his wife, Laura, or Mark Kuch, and I would say: "Peter left my name on the guest list."

I always made sure my name was on the list because that's how I got in for free. Luckily, it was always there. Tommy and Laura would often snicker under their breath that Peter had some kind of crush on me. Although we were very touchy-feely and I often hugged and kissed Peter, it never went beyond that—it was very PG-rated. I see Peter as my very first mentor. Not only did he become a good friend, but because he always saw me taking photos, he helped me turn that passion into a profession.

I often had either a Minolta 35mm camera hung around my neck or I carried a small Kodak 110 instamatic in my pocket. A lot of us teens who paraded through the clubs every night had cameras with us, photographing everything and everyone, and I was fanatical about it.

6

BLACK & WHITE

My obsession with photography started as early as my obsession with music. I had always been a curious kid, and whenever I visited friend's homes, I asked to look at their family photo albums. I loved pictures and seeing what other people's lives looked like. Whenever I visited my Titi Jennie, there was always music playing and at some point during the day I would ask her to bring out the box of family photos. I just wanted to lose myself in them.

In the early seventies, when you went to the neighborhood candy store or pharmacy, there were narrow yellow Kodak 110 instamatic cameras on sale by the cash register. After you took a full round of photos on one of them, you brought it back to that same store and gave them the camera to get the film developed. It wasn't at all like today, when photos and videos are instantaneously available the moment you shoot them on an iPhone or other digital devices.

After they were developed, it wasn't unusual for my simple snapshots to appear grainy and blurry. Those inexpensive Kodak Instamatics often took far from perfect images. But, in the end, that didn't matter to me, because it was more about capturing the moment.

✿   ✿   ✿

One day, Peter Crowley asked me if I wanted to go to Canada with him and the band, Wayne County and the Backstreet Boys. They were heading to the New Yorker Theater in Toronto, to do a Halloween concert. Peter was their manager and he wanted me to be their photographer. I was thrilled, and quickly said yes. For some reason, my mom let me go and I have no idea why. I was only sixteen.

Wayne County was one of the first transgender singers in rock 'n' roll history. At that time, in 1976, she hadn't taken on the name Jayne yet. She was the DJ at Max's before Paul Zone took over, and she introduced everyone to punk rock coming out of England and the U.S.—she knew what was happening before any of the rest of us did. Wayne's band also became the house band at Max's.

We were gone for only about four days and it was a real test for myself as I had never professionally photographed anything before. But I did it, and the most amazing thing was that those photos ended up being published on the cover of *Rock Scene Magazine*. It was my first publication, my first real professional gig, and it was really exciting. When we got back to New York, Peter said to me, "We're recording an EP and we'd like you to shoot the cover."

What was happening? This was way too fast. But apparently, they were on a tight schedule and Peter needed the photo done immediately. I didn't have a second to swallow my fear or be confused at all.

"Can you shoot it right now?" he asked.

My eyes widened. I looked down at the Tri-X film I had in my camera. It had thirty-six exposures and I was at thirty-five. I gulped, nodded, and said my prayers.

I grabbed Wayne.

"Let's hit the toilet."

The toilet was actually a small narrow room that we could barely fit in. Wayne grabbed his guitar, slipped it between his legs, and stuck out his tongue. I took the shot and crossed my fingers.

When I got the photos back from the developers, I held my breath as I quickly looked over the contact sheet. When I found that very last frame, I breathed a huge sigh of relief. The photography gods had been with me that day. It was the last frame in the roll and the image was pure magic.

I took it to Peter and Wayne. They loved it and ended up using it for his first EP, *Blatantly Offenzive*. Between that and the photographs in *Rock Scene Magazine*, I felt more connected to the musicians I loved and the scene that I cherished. I also felt more like a professional photographer. I was sixteen and a path had opened up—though I wasn't sure where it would lead—but there it was, thanks to Peter.

7

10½ INCHES

Everyone has their own scandalous stories about the third floor upstairs at Max's, and I was no exception.

One night, I went up to see Peter and when I walked in, I saw Marc "10½ inch" Stevens,[1] the infamous porn star. He was sitting there with his soon-to-be transsexual wife, Jill Munroe. Peter introduced us and we talked for a bit, then after about a half-hour, Marc sent Jill home and he turned to me and said he thought I was cute.

He ended up asking me to go home with him to his apartment at 72 Bleecker Street. Being a bit of an upstart who thought he knew everything, I had no worries about handling this porn star, who was nearly twenty years older than me.

After we entered his place, he locked the door from the inside with a key and put it inside his pocket. That struck me as strange.

"Take off your clothes," he said, rather seductively.

I was a bit astonished. So, I asked, "May I have something to drink first?"

He brought me a beer and told me he'd be right back. He then disappeared into the bathroom for what seemed like an eternity. When he came out, he was naked and fully erect and asked me if I wanted some cocaine. I shook my head and told him I didn't want any. He told me again to take off my clothes. I panicked, and said: "I don't know if I can do this."

"*Really?*" he said, in a kind of disbelief. "You're here, and we're going to have sex. So, take off your clothes," he demanded.

He was very tough with me, and I was nervous. Then he opened up the drawer of the night table and took out what looked like a small pistol. He placed it on top of the table and then poured out three lines of cocaine. He offered me the coke again. My gut twisted. I turned down the offer and said to him, kind of forcefully, "You know, I want to leave now."

"You're not leaving yet," he insisted.

"If you don't let me leave," I said. "I'm going to wreck your apartment and everyone in the building's gonna hear me!"

I don't know where I got the nerve to say that—I just wanted to get out of there right away.

He became furious, nearly enraged. He put on his underwear and pushed me to the front door and said:

"Get the fuck out of here! You're wasting my fucking time!"

He took out his key, unlocked the door and shoved me out onto the street. It must've been around 3 a.m. I just stood there trembling, wondering how I was going to pull myself together. I was so thrown by the whole situation. It took me about twenty minutes to compose myself and head for the B train back to Brooklyn.

Adventures weren't always trouble-free. In fact, sometimes they could be downright frightening. It still amazes me when thinking about all of the risky situations I've been in that I was never physically hurt, or worse. I had this fearlessness, this gutsiness that I could do anything I wanted to, and I was sure I would be safe. Somehow, luck was on my side—for a little while at least.

8

FLORIDA. BOSTON. NEW YORK.

Around this same time, in 1976, I took a trip to Hollywood, Florida. I had just finished my junior year in high school and I went to visit my cousin Laura and my godmother, Titi Sylvia. Laura had the coolest friends, one being Diane Hensley. As it was my first visit to Florida, I wanted to go out on the town, but none of the girls wanted to take me anywhere. Diane suggested her friend Dennis to show me around. He was a twenty-four-year-old music lover who worked for the U.S. postal service as a mailman, and had a 1976 Corvette convertible.

It was early evening when he picked me at my Titi's house. I heard the car pulling up and by the time I got to the door, he was standing outside in front of his car. When I saw him, he looked so gorgeous and masculine, I was completely thrown, and I hadn't even spoken to him yet.

There was an immediate attraction between us. I didn't think he was gay, but it didn't seem to matter. We drove around that evening, getting to know each other and listening to the Steve Miller Band's album *Fly Like an Eagle*, which eventually became "our" record.

On another night when he came to pick me up, we decided to go to the local drive-in in his convertible to see *Logan's Run*. It was all popcorn and

Jack Daniel's. The moment we got there though, we had to put the top up on the convertible because the mosquitos were eating us alive.

I looked over at Dennis, and he was wearing these gold-rimmed glasses which gave him a very John Lennon vibe that was insanely attractive. When the movie was over, we drove back to his house in Hollywood. Somehow, we ended up in a sleeping bag together. We held each other and it felt very natural. It was so easy and peaceful to fall asleep there with him. We didn't have the word for it then, but what Dennis and I had was a true "bromance."

A bond developed between us that lasted over the next forty years. I was always so excited when I saw his name come up on the telephone, and the first thing he usually said to me was, "How's my New York superstar?"

Dennis became an ordained minister at the Lamb of God Center in Florida. But he struggled with alcohol and drugs his whole life. In 2014, I learned that his kidneys were failing, and that although he had no drugs in his system, he was praying to die. He was on life support for a few days with his family by his side before he passed in August 2014. I know he is now at peace.

❊   ❊   ❊

That happened to me a lot. I found myself in relationships with men who identified themselves as straight. They may have been bisexual, though they rarely admitted to that, and my experiences with them always happened under the guise of secrecy.

> Sexuality is often described as a spectrum; some people identify as entirely straight and others as entirely gay. However, many people lie somewhere in that sizeable grey area between the two . . . [1]

I think it was because I was small and charming, with Farrah Fawcett-like hair, which many men found appealing and non-threatening.

Very late one night, I was cruising the Combat Zone in downtown Boston—the city's adult XXX playground. There were scores of young men hanging out there, going through all the sleazy bars looking to pick up a john to make a few bucks: "The area was infamous for its strip clubs, peep shows, dirty bookstores, booze, drugs, and violence."[2]

I ended up at a small bar with a pool table, where I met a gorgeous blond. His name was Lewis and he had that "just out of prison" look—well-built, with tattoos and brilliant blue eyes.

Actually, he was not a good guy. He told me he was on the run from the law, because, apparently, he had killed a policeman. I never confirmed that had happened, but he said that was why he kept himself under the radar.

A few months later, I went to visit him when he moved to Florida. He lived in a ramshackle cottage with a few other people, not far from the beach. We spent a lot of time near the ocean. We had a visceral, sexual connection and, of course, I wanted to photograph him. We had sex on the beach every night, but we didn't have a lot in common.

After that trip, we stayed in touch by telephone, and then at some point I never heard from him again. It made me wonder if he went back to jail, or if he didn't want to be friends, because I was this innocent kid still in art school. It all felt like a dream, a short moment in time—he was there, and then he wasn't.

✻   ✻   ✻

One summer day, I was walking along Christopher Street. I was still in my teens and all of a sudden, I saw a beautiful, blue Ford pick-up truck, with a blond muscleman sitting in the driver's seat. He was looking out the window and he slowed the truck down as he got closer to me. When I looked over to him, we made eye contact.

He had long, scraggly hair and amazing muscles. The truck came to a full stop right in front of me. He pushed open the passenger door and I got in without a thought. His name was Kip, and he was really hot.

The next thing I knew I was driving with him to Boston, then Provincetown. It was another one of my romps—always with a muscleman, sometimes straight, sometimes gay—all part of my crazy, wonderful journey.

9

ALL THIS AND MORE

While I became a constant presence at Max's, I also took over CBGB's. I had first gone to CBs with my friend Leslie Swiman, who took me there to see Johnny Thunders and the Heartbreakers in 1976. She lived in New Haven, Connecticut, with her family and was a few years older than me. We found each other through our mutual fanaticism for rock 'n' roll.

I saw many bands there, but, ultimately, it was the Dead Boys that mattered the most to me.

The Dead Boys were the house band at CBGB's. Hilly Krystal, the owner of the club, managed them because they were one of the most popular groups on the scene. I went to every single one of their shows.

I adored their loud, "piss-in-your-face" rowdy, hard-core, violent stage antics. They had come out of Youngstown, Ohio—Stiv Bators, Cheetah Chrome, Jimmy Zero, Jeff Magnum and Johnny Blitz. They were pure punk—loud, brash, dirty, fast, and their music blew me away. Stiv, in his rough, cocky way as the lead singer, was also outrageously charming, and I had a wild crush on the drummer, Johnny Blitz (I had a thing for drummers). During this time, I also met Jody Robelo. She was another huge fan of the band and the two of us were forever in the front row at all their shows.

At one point, the guys asked Jody to start a fan club, which is exactly what I had planned to do. Our mutual friend Antone DeSantis brought Jody and me together and it was a love-fest at first sight. Together, we decided to do both the fan club and create a fanzine.

We called the 'zine,' *All this and More*, after one of their songs. It was a cut-and-paste affair of different sized letters and images and was very punk rock. We only ended up doing the one issue because, well, we were kids— we were just going out and having a blast. We weren't focused on "band business," like building up a fan base for the Dead Boys or getting media attention, even though we were dedicated to them. We just wanted to be connected to the band in any way possible.

Because I was always at CBGB's, I was at almost every Ramones show and I became fast friends with Arturo Vega. Arturo was the creator of the legendary Ramones logo and the lighting director for their entire career.

He was tremendously attractive, brilliant, and one of the most demanding and belligerent people I had ever known in my life. He was also my friend for thirty years and shared the same birthday with me—October 13.

We spent so much time together. He visited me regularly when I developed AIDS. He had Thanksgiving dinner with my family—he even became close with my mom during those holidays, endlessly gabbing with her in Spanish.

Arturo and I went to hustler bars and porn clubs all the time and we always dragged our straight friend, Jimmy Marino, with us. But because Arturo and I were two gay men out to have a pretty depraved time, Jimmy sometimes found himself a bit mortified by our antics. He stuck with us anyway because he knew he had no choice and wanted to make sure we all got home in one piece at the end of the night.

One evening, after a Ramones gig, Arturo—who had $22,000 cash in his fanny pack from merchandise sales—decided that we should go out on the town. Jimmy, Arturo, and I piled into a cab to head up to Times Square, where we would end up at Stella's, a bar where young straight men snuggled up to the gay clientele to make a fast buck and pay the rent; or to Cat's, a dive bar where we found ourselves mingling with the rough trade, amid "testosterone-driven theatrics."

Meanwhile, Arturo was so friggin' high that night.

"Arturo!" I said to him. "You have $22,000 cash in your bag and you're not paying attention! Let's go back downtown to the loft, put the money away in the safe, and then we'll go back to Stella's."

So we took the taxi downtown and we had this whole fuckin' to-do in the backseat. When we arrived at Arturo's place on East 2nd Street, we got out, and I noticed that Arturo didn't have the fanny pack with him. We had left the money in the cab! I looked at Jimmy, freaking out.

I ran like a maniac down the street, back to the taxi, and pounded on the trunk.

"We forgot something!" I screamed, though I didn't want the driver to think I was too out of control. Finally, he stopped, and I opened the back door. There was the fanny pack—on the seat! I quickly grabbed it and ran back to Arturo.

Sweating and trying to catch my breath, I handed it to him. He didn't seem very grateful and was a bit obnoxious.

"I *told* you about this!" I said.

Then he opened the fanny pack and started throwing the money all over the street.

"I don't care about this!" he snapped.

I started picking up all the money.

"We're goin' back to the loft now!" I said. When we got there, I put it in a safe in the bedroom although Arturo, of course, had already taken out ten grand—to party with later. That's what it was always like with him—expect the unexpected. From the Ramones gigs to hustler bars to throwing cash in the street. He was crazy, and I adored him.

In mid-2013 Arturo became very ill with liver cancer and ended up at Beth Israel Hospital. Jimmy and I went to go see him and Arturo's family was there, but they wouldn't let us into his room. His nephew, from Chihua-hua, Mexico, was standing guard and said to me: "We don't want you here. He doesn't look good."

"It's a fuckin' hospital!" I shouted. "*Nobody* looks good! But my friend is dying and I'm going to say goodbye to him. You can stay or you can leave, you can do whatever you want, but me and Jimmy are going in to say goodbye."

Arturo heard my voice and he called for us to come into the room. When we went in, we saw he was sitting on top of a closed toilet seat. He waved us into the bathroom and Jimmy and I chuckled while we squeezed in there.

"It's cancer," he said. "and I don't have long."

We hung out with him for a little while but he started to get tired so we gave him a kiss and left so he could rest. Jimmy and I went out to eat and talk about the genius, bossy queen that Arturo was. He died a few days later.

Arturo Vega ·. . . spokesman, logo designer, T-shirt salesman, lighting director and omnipresent shepherd for the Ramones, the speed-strumming punk quartet that helped rejuvenate rock in the mid-1970s, died on June 8 in Manhattan. He was 65.[1]

✿   ✿   ✿

In the middle of 1977, I graduated from City-As-School. I decided to take a year off before planning on college, which Mom seemed okay with though she wasn't very happy about it. She had this certain trust in me and because she was a woman of faith and always prayed that I would be okay, she believed everything would be fine.

As a graduation present, she and my dad gave me enough money to take a trip to Los Angeles with the Dead Boys. The Mumps went along as well because they were the opening act during the short West Coast tour.

That trip was an incredible experience for me. We were there for about a week, bouncing between L.A. and the Old Waldorf in San Francisco. The shows at the Starwood in Los Angeles were legendary and the audience loved them.

When it came time to go north to the San Francisco shows, I rode in the equipment truck with the band's roadies, Scratch and Eugene. I was thrilled with this plan because I was so hot for Eugene. He was gorgeous—a big, strapping cowboy, just the kind of man I liked.

As we were driving north, Scratch kept hounding Eugene to let him drive. Eugene didn't want to do that, because Scratch was always a little out of it. He relented and, sure enough, we were pulled over by the state troopers about a half-hour later. Those cops were real fucks—it seemed like they were looking for a fight. They ended up taking Scratch to jail in Pismo Beach, and Eugene and I continued on to San Francisco.

Later, we checked into the Pacific Motel while the Dead Boys stayed at the Miyako down the street. At one point I had to rush to the pharmacy and get some Kwell lotion for Stiv. He had developed scabies and needed me to swing over to his hotel room and help him into the bathtub, so he could soak in the lotion to get rid of the infestation all over his body. It was kind of gross but I was so happy to be there for him.

Back at the Pacific Motel, I had all these fucking people asking me if they could crash in my room, but I turned them all down because I wanted to be alone with Eugene. There I was again—going for the straight guy.

Later in the evening, Eugene's girlfriend, Candy, showed up. I was super disappointed, but as it turned out, it didn't actually change anything. I got to sleep with Eugene anyway. When I woke up, I found myself lying in-between his legs. I quickly looked around and saw his girlfriend passed out in the next bed. It looked like I dodged a bullet.

When the Dead Boys finished their gigs in San Francisco, they went back to L.A. to do one more show, then to New York before they left on a European tour. I didn't go with them, but before I returned to New York, I went to see Iggy Pop at the Old Waldorf. He wowed the crowd, coming out in a black skin leotard. It was one of the best shows I'd ever seen. Afterwards, I went backstage, where I got a big hug from Iggy and his autograph for my scrapbook. Then he turned around and started talking with Jennifer from the Nuns while I started chatting up Hunt Sales, Iggy's guitar player.

Just like when I insisted on going backstage at *The Rocky Horror Show*— I always got backstage. After the show ended, and everyone left the venue to go home, I was the one who always stayed until last call.

❋   ❋   ❋

During my year off after graduation, I was still living at home, but I was constantly gone. One of my most exciting exploits during this time was an experience I had with Bruce Springsteen.

I went to see him on his "Darkness on the Edge of Town" tour at the Nassau Coliseum in the summer of 1978. I was so excited. I felt the same fevered energy for Bruce that I had for Patti Smith. I had first seen him at the Palladium in 1976 with my friend Leslie on his "Lawsuit Tour." I actually got to meet him then at the stage door, where he autographed my scrapbook.

This time was a little different. Before the concert started, I went into the Coliseum's backstage area. I didn't have an all-access pass, but no one stopped me—very different from today when you're frisked the moment you approach backstage.

I looked around and knocked on the first door I saw and there was Bruce, alone, sitting quietly at a table. I went in and said, "Hi—I don't know if you remember me, but we met when you played the Palladium in 1976. My name is Michael Alago, and I'm a huge fan."

He smiled back.

"That's really nice," he said. "But I only have twenty minutes before I have to get on stage."

"Of course," I said. Then I looked closer at him. "You don't look very happy, though."

He lifted his head and said, "Well, I have this hangnail and it really hurts." He reached out his hand and showed me his thumb.

Instinctively, I leaned forward, and I was about to bite off the nail, when he gave me a worried look, so I stopped and said to him, "Uh, we can take that off real easy."

I tugged lightly at it and after a minute pulled it completely off.

"Thanks!" he said. He looked really relieved. I guess it had been seriously hurting.

Suddenly, the tour manager came in and I swiftly pushed the nail into my pocket. He seemed quite anxious as it was only minutes before the show was supposed to start.

"What's goin' on here? "Where's your pass?"

"I don't have a pass," I said.

"Well, you have to leave!" he shouted. But then, with even more balls than I thought I had, I said to him, "Excuse me, but could you take a picture of us together first?" and I handed him my camera.

"Who is this kid?" he said to Bruce, but he ended up taking the picture of us anyway.

"Thank you," I quickly said, because he looked like he was about to grab me by the neck, so I raced out and back to my seat, feeling around madly for Bruce's hangnail in my pocket.

I ended up taping the nail into my scrapbook, but somehow, after many years, it slipped out and disappeared. My love and admiration for Bruce, however, has remained as strong as ever.

10

MULTIPLE EXPOSURE

In September of 1978, I started at the School of Visual Arts. I set my major as photography, which just seemed natural. I had a lot of fun with the program except that my main photography professor, Alice Beck-Odette, didn't like what I was doing. She didn't feel the photographs I was taking were "real" or "good" or "valid," and it was very unnerving.

I was shooting photos of shows at CBGB's, Max's Kansas City, The Bottom Line, the Palladium, as well as all the downtown dive bars where bands would perform. Many of the images were unexpected, and surprising. I started developing my own photographs in the darkroom and it felt like the pictures I was creating were very powerful, but the SVA faculty disagreed. I only stayed there for a year.

In the summer of 1979, my friend Roseanne Fontana introduced me to a guitar player—her friend Mitch from Elmont, New York. Roseanne knew I wanted to start a band and thought Mitch and I would get along. Mitch introduced me to a bunch of his friends—Tommy, Irwin and Johnny—and we started rehearsing in his living room.

I became the lead singer and Mitch was the guitar player. We got a set of cover songs together from "My Sharona" to "Pump it Up" to "Wild Horses," and we called ourselves Multiple Exposure. We played all over Long Island, at bars like The Empty Can and The Winner's Circle. We also wrote songs together and had a great time.

We usually opened our set with the song "Palisades Park," which I started using after seeing Blondie perform it. I wrote the lyrics for a bunch of our own songs as well. The band only lasted about six months, though. It wasn't a devastating end; it just petered out.

I then started performing on my own. I had been following the works of Gil Scott Heron, Patti Smith, The Last Poets, John Rechy and James Purdy from a very young age. They gave me the inspiration to write on my own. I decided to perform my words live and booked some poetry shows. I titled it *Scatterbrain* and performed around the city at places like the Savoy, Peppermint Lounge, Youthanasia (the Androgyny Party), The Ritz, and CBGB's.

> *Cocaine and gardenias = fame*
> Hollyweed. Hollywood at the time.
> Platinum blonde behind ebon shades.
> A little girl weeps hysterically.
> A woman cries for love, security, desire and fear of madness.
> The ocean was her best friend. (So was champagne)
> The freedom to drift with the sea and the sands
> Gave her great pleasure.
> You had an affair with the camera.
> Being so greatly loved, sometimes worried you.
> You always gave your all, even though you thought
> It wasn't enough.
> Gosh. I love you.
> Damn, we need you
> The photos are embedded in my brain.
> Hey Marilyn, something's got to give.[1]

✿   ✿   ✿

While I continued performing live, I was working in the Shipping & Receiving department at the District 65 Pharmacy on Astor Place, where I had started about six months previously. One Saturday, when I was visiting my dad at his office, I went for a walk down East 11th Street, and I happened to notice a sign on a nearby building that read, "Video Club Opening Résumés Being Accepted." I wondered what in the world that could be. What was a *video club*?

11

THE RITZ

The building was the old Webster Hall. It was built in 1886 and had a long history as a nightclub, entertainment and concert hall. In the thirties and forties, it had been a speakeasy of sorts, when prohibition was flatly ignored. In 1980, it was owned by Casa Galicia, a cultural organization representing the people of Galicia, Spain.

For me, it was The Wizard of Oz. The deco architecture of the main hall was intoxicating. When I entered, I was swept up by the grandeur of the space. Suddenly, I looked up. Standing in the ornate balcony surrounding the hall, a man was watching me. It turned out to be Jerry Brandt, the wizard himself.

Jerry was a true icon in the music world. Having started at the William Morris Agency, he discovered Carly Simon, The Voices of East Harlem, Jobriath, and helped bring the Rolling Stones to the United States. And, in 1980, he was at Webster Hall, planning to open the first rock club that had a twenty-foot screen, showcasing the hottest new videos. It would be called The Ritz.

I waved up to him.

"We're not even open yet kid," he said. "What can I help you with?"

"I want a job!" I said

"Do you have a résumé?"

"No," I told him. "I work in a pharmacy and go to the School of Visual Arts."

For some reason, he was amused and he asked me up to his office.

We immediately connected and started talking everything music—from the Great American Songbook to the popular music of the day. As we continued our conversation, Jerry realized how much I knew about the New York music scene and who were the hottest up-and-coming acts. Jerry said, along with my vast musical knowledge, I had a sparkle in my eye that he liked, and he hired me immediately.

"You're going to get my coffee, open my mail, and screen all my phone calls."

I couldn't believe my ears. I was being hired to work in the music business. My dreams were starting to come true.

Every afternoon, after I finished at the pharmacy, I dashed over to The Ritz, brought Jerry his coffee, and assisted him with everything.

During that process, I was privy to all of his conversations with booking agents, reviewing the monthly schedule of bands, and going over the budget. I asked a ton of questions. I was a quick study and, very soon, I became the assistant booker.

I worked with Jerry in bringing in everyone from PiL to Divine to the Misfits, U2, Ray Charles, Jerry Lee Lewis, BB King, the historic return of Tina Turner, Prince, The Police, Siouxsie and the Banshees, and many others.

✿   ✿   ✿

About 6 months after I started, tragedy hit the rock 'n' roll world. On December 8, 1980, John Lennon was returning from a recording session with Yoko Ono for what would be the *Double Fantasy* album, when he was shot and killed outside of his home, The Dakota. It felt like a kick in the heart for everyone. I was numb, and so was the rest of the world. We really didn't know how to process it—why anyone would want to kill such a gentle spirit, a true icon—it sucked the life out of all of us.

A few weeks after Lennon's death, Jerry's phone rang at The Ritz, and I picked it up.

"Jerry Brandt's office, how may I help you?" I said.

"Hi, it's Yoko Ono. I would like to speak with Mr. Brandt."

"Of course," I said, and I quickly transferred the call to Jerry.

Yoko was aware of The Ritz as a new, unique club and she wanted to premiere a video of her song "Walking on Thin Ice."

We were certainly surprised to hear from her that soon and equally surprised that she had begun working on a promotional video so shortly after John's death. The video included clips of their family life, intimate moments of them in bed, and powerful images of her walking defiantly down 72nd Street, near their home.

Being the emotional artist Yoko is, I believe she was using her creativity to work through her unimaginable grief. Not only was John carrying the tape of "Walking on Thin Ice" when he was murdered, but it was the first time since 1964 that he had used his Beatles Rickenbacker on a recording, and it was also the last song on which he ever played a guitar solo.

The Ritz had become known everywhere as a revolutionary nightclub because it was the first to feature a huge video screen in the front of the main hall. Yoko wanted to debut the video of John on that screen because she felt it would get the most attention there. It was an inspiring gift, and heartbreaking to watch. The video was so important because it kept John's spirit alive for Yoko, their family, and all the rest of us—his loving fans.

❊   ❊   ❊

A few months later, I booked Bow Wow Wow, a new band created by Malcolm McLaren, previously the manager of the Sex Pistols. He had pulled together a few members of Adam and the Ants to create the band, and added a young, spunky, unknown thirteen-year-old singer named Anabella Lwin. McLaren had discovered her when she was singing in a local laundry shop.

Bow Wow Wow was scheduled to headline at The Ritz, and it was going to be a huge weekend because it would be their U.S. debut. It was a sold-out event. I felt even more certain about what a great job I was doing at the club.

But a week before the band was scheduled to arrive, McLaren called and said they had to cancel. I was completely thrown. What the fuck? McLaren told me that Lwin's mother objected to having her thirteen-year-old daughter travel overseas. I started to panic. I was becoming furious with him. I shouted over the phone that we would pay for her mother to accompany her to New York City. I promised to provide whatever she needed to make it happen—*any* accommodations, *anything*. But her mother wouldn't budge—she wouldn't give permission to allow Annabella to travel. They weren't coming.

I totally freaked out—everybody in the office totally freaked out. We had sold three thousand tickets for a two-night event. How were we going to tell the owners of the club—the Leibowitz brothers—that we suddenly had no show and would have to return everyone's money?

I wasn't sure what to do. My brain started working overtime. We had a sold-out weekend with no entertainment. I had to think quickly, now that Bow Wow Wow had totally blown us off.

Then suddenly, I remembered Public Image Limited was in town on a press junket for their new album release, *Flowers of Romance.*

I called Liz Rosenberg, head of publicity at Warner Bros. The stars were definitely aligning for me, because the band just happened to be in her office at the moment I called. I made them aware of the Bow Wow Wow cancellation and that I thought it would be an awesome idea to have PiL perform in their place that weekend. I asked if I could send a car for them to have a meeting with Jerry and me to discuss how we could make the event happen.

After a few hours back and forth, we came to some kind of agreement with the band. Meanwhile, they had arrived in the U.S. with no instruments because they were only here to do press for their new album. We had to think fast because we only had forty-eight hours before the show. We talked about renting a Prophet 5 Synthesizer for Keith Levene, so he could program music into it. They knew about the twenty-foot white video screen, and they loved the experimental performance aspect of it all.

After we settled everything, and once word got out that PiL were appearing, it became the talk of the town. We got WLIR to promote ticket giveaways, and the excitement in the air was over the top. Both nights quickly sold out.

PiL intend to . . . be up on stage, but they plan to spend the show completely behind a twenty foot by twenty-foot video screen . . . Behind that screen the set up almost looks normal . . . There's a drum kit, a synthesizer bank, a few guitars and basses, two video cameras and a record player . . . They could play records, play white noise, make shadow puppets, tell jokes, even, for all we know, play a set—but the key thing seems to be that from no vantage point out front will anyone be able to see any of PiL in the flesh.[1]

Little did we know, however, that the evening would turn into a violent free-for-all. At the start of the show, the song "Flowers of Romance" blasted through the speakers, but five minutes later, you could feel that something was not right.

John and the band refused to come out in front of the screen. PiL saw this event as a performance art piece, but the fans wanted to see a concert. They wanted to hear the band play and play furiously—basically, they wanted Johnny Rotten in action.

But they didn't get that, and the audience went ballistic. They threw bottles at the huge video screen. Chairs flew everywhere. The crowd pulled on the screen, tearing it down, ripping holes in it and smashing bottles on the stage.

John still refused to come out front, because to him, this was not a gig. He periodically played improvised parts of PiL songs, which infuriated the crowd.

The agitated audience starting hissing and booing, giving PiL the middle finger, screaming: "Fucking rush the Stage!"

"Fuck you, Keith"

John kept aggressively teasing the audience: "Am I wonderful? Are you getting your money's worth?"

He continued in an obnoxious tone: "It's so nice to be in your wonderful city! You're what I call a passive audience!"

The crowd screamed back: "Fuck you!"[2]

I was shocked as I watched from the balcony, and Jerry was livid. As the crowd completely trashed the place, Jerry furiously marched backstage; I followed him. Jerry insisted that John perform for the crowd, but he refused. Finally, Jerry closed down the show and the club for the whole weekend. In the end, it was a combination of John's ego, sarcasm, and cynicism that created the mayhem. The local news went wild, as did the international music papers:

> That anything came together at all was the mastermind of Michael Alago, a slight, pretty and effeminate man who books The Ritz. . . . Public Image Ltd . . . obliterated those boundaries between theater and real life, between the mock violence and the implied threat of the Dead Kennedys or the Sex Pistols and the real desire of an audience to destroy a band and everything they stood for, and the encouragement of the band for them to do so.[3]

After the show, a bunch of us, including photographer Laura Levine, gathered in the dressing room. Scott Rubinoff, a big PiL fan, whose head was bleeding from the crowd's attack earlier, was there as well—he was so excited to meet John. We all drank up a storm, celebrating the chaos of the show. An unpredictable but lovely thing came out of it for me as well—a close, personal, and professional friendship with John Lydon—one that lasts to this day.

> Public Image Ltd. is still remembered for a 1981 New York City show at The Ritz (now Webster Hall), where it performed behind a screen, with Mr. Lydon taunting the audience, until the crowd rioted, hurling beer bottles and pulling down the stage set. Band revivals are good box office, as Mr. Lydon knows from his Sex Pistols reunions. But this PiL is no joke."[4]

✿　　✿　　✿

The following fall, I went to the UK to scout out bands to perform at The Ritz. I was there for a few weeks and I saw Bauhaus, Altered Images, the

Thompson Twins, Theater of Hate, The Cramps, and Echo and the Bunnymen at a Festival in Leeds, as well as Depeche Mode on *Top of the Pops* in London.

One night I went to the club Heaven, under Charing Cross Road, to see Divine perform, when I was joined by Stiv Bators.

We ended up standing at the bar, having a long talk. Stiv was pretty depressed. He didn't know what he should do as a performer outside of the Dead Boys. He wasn't sure if he wanted to return to the States or stay in Europe and continue playing with his new band, Lords of the New Church. He was involved with a woman in London and complained that women were always his downfall.

Suddenly, we felt the presence of a bunch of skinheads circling us. They started calling us "poofs"—British slang for faggots. Being from Brooklyn, I wasn't going to take any of their shit. Glaring at them, I said, "There's no problem here, guys."

Stiv and I finished our beers and I whispered to him, "Let's piss in our beer mugs!"

We quickly turned around, whipped out our cocks, and pissed in the mugs. Then we offered the two mugs to the skinheads as a peace offering. They took huge gulps of what they thought was beer and at that moment I said to Stiv:

"Get ready to run!"

We thought this was hilarious, but of course we didn't want to get our asses kicked either. The skinheads spit out the piss and sneered at us. We immediately swung around and ran backstage into Divine's dressing room, slammed the door, and locked it.

Divine was painting on his last eyebrow. He turned and looked at us. "What kind of trouble are you in now?"

We fell onto the ground, grabbing our stomachs, laughing until it hurt.

12

WAR ZONE

Late in the fall of 1982, I finally got my own apartment. All of this time, I had been living at home on New Utrecht Avenue and that was becoming more than complicated. I had been gone—emotionally—from Brooklyn, my mother, and my sister for a long time. However, I hadn't physically moved out yet. Maybe that was a comfort to my mom, or even me, I don't know. But I was going to be twenty-three years old soon and I had to go. I needed to move into the city.

I moved in with my friend Roseanne to an apartment at 380 East 10th Street. It was between Avenues B and C, and the center of Lower East Side decay. It was before the Koch heroin busts throughout the city,[1] so bodegas and delis sold coke and pot and whatever drug you wanted. One time a car flipped over on East 9th Street and it stayed there for two weeks—completely upside down. No one in the city government, or the sanitation department, gave a shit—they couldn't be bothered to flip it back over and haul it away. Those streets were filled with nasty garbage and rot everywhere.

The apartment we moved into was a large studio with a small shower stall in the kitchen and a bamboo screen set up in the middle, so we could each have our own space. Privacy, though, was a joke but neither of us seemed to mind, and I even brought home a different guy almost every other night. Luckily, Roseanne didn't care.

Often when I left work at The Ritz at 4 a.m. and had a couple of hits of coke in me, I sauntered over to The New St. Marks Baths, located at 6 St. Marks Place in the East Village. Without a care in the world and with some real bravado, I usually cut to the front of a very long line stretching from the door of the bath house, down the street to 3rd Avenue. I would then give my money to the attendant at the front desk and get a key to a private room, where I usually met up with a hot stud from Staten Island named Guy. He was built like a brick shithouse, was wildly handsome, and had what looked like a Brillo pad for a toupee. From our first encounter, we were intensely attracted to each other and that manifested itself in heavy make-out sessions, hand jobs, and a quick release. I would then leave his room, hit the showers, and head home as the sun was coming up—completely satisfied.

About a month after Roseanne and I moved in, we were robbed. The strange thing was that the thieves only took my stuff—my stereo, my television, and most of my newly bought clothes from King's Road on my London trip. In fact, they left Roseanne's television on the floor—like they had taken it off her shelf, looked at it, then decided it wasn't good enough, and dumped it on the floor. After another couple months, we were robbed again and I decided I couldn't take it anymore—particularly since it was always *my* stuff the thieves wanted. So, until I could find another place, I moved in with Danny Fields in his large West Village apartment.

✿   ✿   ✿

Danny joined the staff at The Ritz not long after I started working there, and we became close very quickly. He was funny and brilliant and the budding friendship with this historic guy in rock 'n' roll thrilled me.

He broke into the industry working for Elektra Records, first doing publicity for the Doors, then signing both Iggy Pop's band the Stooges and the MC5 (on the same day), which would ultimately lead to his managing the Ramones. You could make a convincing case that without Danny Fields, punk rock wouldn't have happened.[2]

Certainly, life in The Ritz office could be a little intimidating. Both Jerry and Danny had been instrumental in rock 'n' roll since the sixties, and I found myself having to forge my own way. I was grateful that I got to learn so much from these two great men.

One time, Black Flag was playing the Ritz and both Danny and I had a crush on their lead singer, Henry Rollins. On the afternoon before the first show, the band came in to do a soundcheck and wound up performing a full-on concert level work-out. When the soundcheck was over, we noticed the gym shorts and T-shirt Henry was wearing were soaked with sweat. He came up to our office and plopped down in a chair. Danny and I looked at each other. We were about to go mental. Henry started chatting us up and the moment he stood up to leave, Danny and I both dove into the chair to smell it. It was very Spinal Tap—"Smell the glove!"

When I moved into Danny's, I set up a corner in the living room with a small mattress and a sleeping bag. It wasn't home, but it was cozy.

One night while I was living there, I went out to Danceteria to see Alan Vega, then I went to CBGB's to see The Lordz—they had a really cute drummer named Vic. He had a super-tight body and I went nuts for him. I got him drunk but there were too many people around him all the time, so I didn't get a chance to seduce him and drag him home.

I was really fuckin' high when I got back to Danny's house, and a whole gang of guys—Danny, Steve, Joel, and Mitchell—were there. They were starting to have an orgy, piling on top of each other, when suddenly Danny disappeared into his room. I ended up having sex with Joel, then with Mitchell. I found Mitchell very hot and exciting. He had a hard, muscular body and we had a wonderful time together.

The next day, Mitchell came back over and we hung out and talked.

"You know, I've never really been into that orgy scene," he said.

I laughed.

"Yeah, me neither."

We talked about music and went out to get something to eat, then we went back to his apartment. We listened to the new Rickie Lee Jones album, *Pirates*, and had sex. Initially, I wasn't sure what I was feeling about Mitchell, but I sensed that I wanted to be around him more and that I didn't want to stop. Eventually, our connection became very deep, and we started dating exclusively. That ended up causing enormous change in my life because I learned, after I had been with him for a while, that his father was a record executive and was in the process of restarting Elektra Records.

A couple months later, Lori Reese and I moved into a building at 242 Mulberry Street, in Little Italy. It was a one-bedroom, and when we first got there, boy, did it need some major cleaning! But I was really excited about the place. It was also directly across the street from the Ravenite Social Club, the headquarters for the Gambino Crime family, where John Gotti reigned.

Not long after we moved in, I got a call from Geffen Records. They were looking for an A&R rep for their New York office. I guess I had become a bit of a hot shot, booking all these exciting new and established bands at The Ritz and, as Jerry always said, I had my ear to the ground. So, it wasn't surprising that someone at Geffen called me in for an interview, nonetheless I was floored. After I got off the phone, I started fantasizing about going out to California and meeting everyone at the Geffen offices, which was a series of bungalows on Sunset Boulevard.

I had been feeling worn out at The Ritz—work was 24/7. I ached to just get away—a vacation, anything—so getting that call from Geffen seemed like it happened at the right time. A few days later, I met with John Kalodner from the label. It went really well, and I was set to go to L.A. to meet with the man himself, David Geffen.

In the end, they didn't hire me. Inexperience was the red flag, though I think they liked the idea of me, since I was so close and active with every major band that came through New York. More than anything, the fact that I didn't get the Geffen job wasn't the point. What I knew was it was the beginning of the end for me at The Ritz.

Anthony Alago, U.S. Air Force, 1955.
(Author Collection)

Blanche and Tony's wedding
picture, November 15, 1958.
(Author Collection)

11/25/58

It was so nice
to be remembered by you
and from the bottom of
our hearts we thank you
for the lovely gift
and the good
wishes.

Blanche + Tony

Blanche in Brooklyn, 1960
(Author Collection)

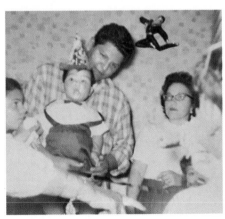

Second Birthday with Mom and Dad
in Brooklyn, 1961(Author Collection)

Me, Mom, and Dad, Chauncey Street, 1962.
(Author Collection)

Abuela Ursula in Brooklyn, 1960
(Author Collection)

First Grade, Our Lady of
Lourdes School, 1965.
(Author Collection)

Titi Jennie, Brooklyn, 1961.
(Author Collection)

Me and Cheryl, Brooklyn, 1969.
(Author Collection)

Me, Matthew, and Gloria Alago,
New York City, 2018.
(Author Collection)

Alice Cooper Concert Edition Program,
Madison Square Garden, NYC, 1973.
(Author Collection)

With Alan Vega, Max's Kansas City,
New York City, 1976. (Author Collection)

Marc Stevens, 'Mr. 10½ inches,'
Adult Film Star (www.therialtoreport.com)

Wayne County & the Electric Chairs,
Blatantly Offenzive EP Cover, 1978.
(© Michael Alago)

Backstage at The Rocky Horror Show *on Broadway with Tim Curry and Meatloaf, 1975. (© Sunny Bak)*

Opening night ticket stub, A Chorus Line, *1975. (Author Collection)*

Danny Papa, Brooklyn, early 1970s. (© Michael Alago)

The Rocky Horror Show *Advertisement, 1975. (Author Collection)*

Dennis Bremser snapshot, Hollywood, Florida, 1976. (© Michael Alago)

Dennis Bremser combing his hair, Hollywood, Florida, 1976. (© Michael Alago)

Self Portrait with Lewis, Homestead, Florida, 1978. (© Michael Alago)

With Dead Boys' drummer Johnny Blitz,
Tropicana Hotel, West Hollywood, CA, 1977.
(Author Collection)

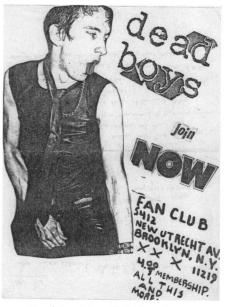

Dead Boys' Fan Club Flyer, 1977.
(Author Collection)

Dead Boys' Stiv Bators, CBGB, 1977.
(© Michael Alago)

Dead Boys' Cheetah Chrome,
CBGB, 1977. (© Michael Alago)

Patti Smith, Central Park Schaefer Music Festival, 1976. (© Michael Alago)

Lori Reese and Patti Smith, Central Park Schaefer Music Festival, 1976. (© Michael Alago)

At Max's Kansas City, New York City, 1977. (Photo courtesy of Paul Zone, from the book "PLAYGROUND: Growing Up In The New York Underground" By Paul Zone, Published by Glitterati Editions.)

13

RED PARROT

Jerry started bringing in other people to the office to share in the booking activities. Maybe he sensed I was feeling itchy—that I had a hunger for something else. So, while I continued working there, I started booking bands every Wednesday night at the Red Parrot nightclub.

Yet, in early 1983, I finally left The Ritz. Between speaking to Mitchell about his father's plans for restarting Elektra and my desire to do more in the music business, it felt right to move on. Bill Brusca, the day manager at The Ritz, happened to be leaving the club at the same time and, luckily, he got me that weekly booking gig at the Red Parrot, which meant I could stay employed while I waited hopefully for an interview with Mitchell's father, Bob Krasnow.

❋　　❋　　❋

The Red Parrot opened in 1982 and was located on 57th Street and 11th Avenue near the West Side Highway. One of the more striking things about the place was that, once you entered, there were a dozen huge climate-controlled cylinders housing large, beautiful red parrots.

I ended up bringing in a lot of exceptional acts to the club, including Madonna, Ronnie Spector, David Johansen, Bow Wow Wow, Divine, James Brown, and George Clinton. I also arranged for silk-screened posters to be designed by the performance artist, John Sex.[1] Every week he screened a hundred posters for each show and we pasted them up all over the city.

One night, when I showed up at the club for work, Wayland Flowers and Madame were in the dressing room as they were appearing that evening. Wayland was a comedian and puppeteer who had risen to fame in the seventies largely due to his buddy—an off-color, wooden puppet named Madame. Wayland described Madame as "my mama, my grandmother, my aunt and a lot of people I had watched in the movies. She's Mammy Yokum to Marlene Dietrich to Marjorie Main."[2]

I went backstage to make sure Wayland had everything he needed and when I opened the door, I found him so high on cocaine, I was afraid he wouldn't be able to perform. I looked at him and he shot back a nasty stare then threw Madame on the floor. I was mortified. That was his ticket, that craggy old puppet is what shot him to fame on *The Andy Williams Show* and *Hollywood Squares*, and he had just thrown her on the ground. I feared he might step all over her, so I picked her up and put her gently down on a chair. Eventually, we had to wait until he came down from all the coke in his system, because he could barely speak and we couldn't cancel, as the event was sold out.

The Red Parrot was a blast to work at and, for one weekend, I was able to get Jerry Lee Lewis booked. He demanded that a 50 percent deposit of his fee be sent to his home in Georgia, which I did. Then the day before he was set to arrive, he canceled. It turned out he had surgery on his butt and couldn't make it. Meanwhile, the weekend was sold out. I thought I might lose it, and I said to his agent in a frantic phone call: "I will provide a perfect pillow for him to stick under his ass. Just get him up here!"

"Mr. Lewis is not coming," he insisted.

"Ok, fine!" I said. "Just send back the 50 percent deposit." His agent said he would—except he never did. The club owner, Jimmy Murray, wanted Bill Brusca to repay the deposit, which Lewis never returned. Bill freaked out so he got hold of a gorgeous escort for Jimmy, and Jimmy let him off the hook. "A hot trick cures everything," Bill said.

Chuck Berry and James Brown also insisted on a 50 percent deposit up front or they would be no-shows.

James Brown played the club in March 1983 and the thing I remember most about that evening was when some I.R.S. agents showed up to get the money we were paying Brown, because he owed back taxes to the government. Except we had paid him in advance.

All the old-school black entertainers wanted 50 percent sent to them upfront and the remainder in cash prior to the gig. They had been screwed out of money too many times. The bias and prejudice against blacks in the fifties and sixties was as prominent in music as it was in the rest of the country, and they never forgot it.

Often catapulted to success from a neighborhood street corner or, like Little Richard, from a bus terminal kitchen where he was washing dishes, black musicians seldom had access to good advice about record contracts, royalty payments, marketing, promotion, or career development. As a result, they were routinely swindled out of their publishing rights and underpaid for record sales.[3]

When the show was over, Brown and his band rushed up to the roof and down the fire escape to dodge the I.R.S. agents.

Chuck Berry performed a few months earlier and he required a "pick-up" band to back him up. In those cases, I usually hired Arno Hecht and the Uptown Horns. Chuck always wanted to pay the band the least amount of money as possible, and when he arrived in his dressing room, I had to have the last 50 percent of his fee in cash, with a bottle of Grand Marnier. Every time I booked him, there were different women with him and they were always white. Before he went onstage, all three of us—Chuck, his lady friend of the moment, and me—stood there counting the remaining 50 percent of his fee. When it was definite that it was all there, the young lady put it in her purse and Chuck went onstage.

Aside from all that, Chuck was really nice and sat at the bar with me having drinks before his gig. My dad was a big Chuck Berry fan and he came to both the early and late shows. He never came to any of the concerts I promoted. But he was such a huge Chuck Berry fan, that when he showed up for those shows, I got a chance to introduce him to Chuck and I was delighted. I think Dad specifically came to these shows because I was never around the family anymore, and this was a chance for us to get together and bond.

During those spectacular Wednesday night concert series, I also booked Madonna, whose self-titled debut album was just being released. She was still doing track dates, so I had her perform her singles "Everybody" and "Burning Up." I had spoken with her agent, Rob Light at ICM, and argued about whether I was going to pay her $2,000 or $2,500 for the gig. I ended up paying her the $2,500. The New York City night life came out in droves to hear her. That evening, we had a number of special guests in the house, including Afrika Bambaataa, Robert Mapplethorpe, and Bernard Summer, the lead singer from New Order, who I was so in love with that after I gave him a hit of ecstasy, I proposed marriage—another amazing Wednesday night.

14

ELEKTRA RECORDS

In February of 1983, I found myself sitting in Bob Krasnow's office at Elektra Records in the Rolex building at 665 Fifth Avenue. I was there to interview for an A&R job, which was a bit bizarre to me, because I wasn't sure what an A&R person did. I sat on a rather plush sofa near the receptionist's desk. As I waited, my nerves started to get the best of me.

Bob Krasnow was the new chairman of Elektra. He had recently taken over the company that year and was starting with an empty slate, building a staff from scratch and, to my surprise and shock, I was one of the first people he was interviewing for his A&R department.

Mitchell—whom I had been dating for a few months by that point—had referred me to his dad. In fact, when I talked about my increasing desire to move forward in my career, Mitchell suggested I meet with him. I had been booking bands for three years and I was anxious for something else—but I had no idea what that was—where was I going?

From a young, excitable fan, Jerry Brandt created a professional out of me. I absorbed every single bit of information from Jerry that I could and I became the best assistant ever. But as I began booking more and more national acts, I knew there had to be more to the business. I just didn't know what that "more" was.

The Elektra reception room felt a bit cold. I started to think I couldn't get through this interview. Suddenly, I noticed there was a lot of contemporary art on the walls. Mitchell had told me his father was a big art collector and, when I looked around, I saw a life-sized masked sculpture made of refuse by David Finn; a glass, framed, original yellow suit from the band, Devo; a Joni Mitchell woven tapestry; and, a very cartoon-like Leslie Lew painting of children playing 45 rpm records.

I was getting excited. I loved art and I knew a lot about it, especially the current stars exhibiting downtown at that time. I decided I would talk to Krasnow about Haring, Schnabel, and Basquiat—they were the New York fixtures I was most familiar with. In fact, a few months previously, I had danced under the Basquiat mural in the Mike Todd room at the Palladium.

After a few minutes, Krasnow appeared. He wasn't as tall as I thought he would be, but he was impeccably dressed in a gorgeous dark Italian suit with a black, silk tie and a white shirt radiating deep power. He was partially bald with perfectly angled grey hair and an unlit cigar balanced between his fingers. My initial thought upon seeing him was he had a very strong, stern face that could easily shout out a harsh command at any moment, for any reason.

He reached out his hand to me and as he did, the cufflinks on his wrist fell into a haze of diamonds and gold.

I immediately stood up, shook his hand and returned an uneasy smile. I felt a bit awkward in my black jeans and T-shirt (although I wore a pair of dress shoes, not my sneakers) but I was there, and I was going to get through this—somehow.

He showed me into his office which was larger than my entire one-room apartment and had a wall of windows overlooking Fifth Avenue. I sat down and immediately noticed he had a Terry Winters and a Robert Longo on his walls.

"By the way, have you gone to the Haring exhibit at the Tony Shafrazi Gallery?" I asked him.

"Yes," he replied. "I like him very much." He lit his cigar and smiled at me.

Within minutes, we were ripping through the current art world with excitement. When we paused a little while later, we dove head-on into everything music.

Bob was a maverick in the music world since the early sixties when he did promotion work for James Brown. In 1968, he started Blue Thumb Records with Tommy Lipuma and Don Graham, bringing in The Pointer Sisters, Dave Mason, and Captain Beefheart while helping launch many other acts, including Ike & Tina Turner. I told him about my music obsession which started when I went to my first concert in 1973 to see Alice Cooper, and we began discussing the history of music from The Great American Song Book to Captain Beefheart, David Bowie and Marvin Gaye—we ran the spectrum of the hottest artists at that moment. If there was one thing I absolutely couldn't hide, it was my lust for music. All music.

After about an hour, Bob stood up, shook my hand, said he really enjoyed our conversation and that he would be in touch. I turned and smiled to his executive assistant, Ruth, as I walked out the door. When I reached the elevator, I wiped my eyebrows and prayed—I really wanted that job.

✿　　✿　　✿

A few weeks later, while I was working on my Wednesday and Thursday night schedules at the Red Parrot, I got a call from Krasnow.

"I'm going to hire you," he announced.

I was stunned, and thanked him as professionally as I could. When we hung up, tears started forming in my eyes. I couldn't believe this turn in my life, and the problem was, I had no idea what an A&R executive did.

✿　　✿　　✿

Those first six months were a huge learning curve. Bob pulled me into his office to sit in on phone calls with agents, managers, and lawyers.

There I was, a twenty-three-year-old nightclub assistant director and suddenly I was thrust into a corporate environment. Bob was aware that a major bottom line needed to be satisfied for our parent company, Time Warner. However, the brilliance of Krasnow was that he knew how to merge art and commerce successfully. What Bob was doing was grooming me in how to approach record deals with the same finesse that he did so beautifully.

The primary job of the A&R department makes up the backbone of every record company label. The role of the A&R executive is to find and acquire new talent because without extraordinary and potentially bankable artists there is no label. Then the A&R executive nurtures and develops the new talent to the point when it's time to go into the recording studio. They oversee the recording process by finding a producer, developing a budget, and making sure all of the songs are top-notch. I was just praying I could do *any* of this.

When I was given my own office, I was beside myself with excitement. I was anxious to set it up perfectly. I hung some of my black-and-white photography collection on the walls—a Mapplethorpe, an Albert Sanchez of Dolph Lundgren in the swimming pool at the Beverly Hills Hotel painted by David Hockney. and a Peter Beard of Truman Capote visiting Bobby Beausoleil in San Quentin prison. I also put up a very colorful Ted Rosenthal poster of an Italian exhibition of his sculptures. Art was a world Bob and I shared with great passion. If you had the opportunity to visit his home, you were greeted at the front door by a silver life-sized double-image Elvis Presley by Warhol. I believe it was the only double that existed. Bob exposed me to more intellectually stimulating and refined works than I could ever have imagined.

Often, when Bob knocked on your office door you would be presented with completely unexpected surprises. Once, he tapped on mine and opened it and Andy Warhol was standing right next to him. Warhol introduced himself and gave me the latest copy of *Interview* magazine, which he signed. I thanked him, trying not to faint from the shock. Bob did that with everyone in the office.

As I became more involved in my job, I listened to thousands of demo tapes investigating potential bands to sign. I traveled constantly to wherever there was an artist whose sound sparked my interest—Austin, Dallas, Memphis, Boston, New Orleans, San Francisco, Los Angeles, and every so often I would head north to my one of my other favorite cities, Toronto. All those places were thriving with up-and-coming, unsigned bands from every genre.

That was the job: searching, speculating, judging—hoping I would find the next big thing.

15

AMERICAN DREAMER

I think it helped me when I started working at Elektra, that I had seriously diverse tastes. It was like that when I began diving into the music scene in the seventies—from Alice Cooper to Aretha Franklin, to *Rocky Horror* on Broadway, and Suicide. That impulse found me checking out and bringing into the company many unexpected and surprising artists.

The Cars had been on the Elektra label since their debut self-titled album was released in 1978. By 1983, they were making the label millions of dollars, and Ric Ocasek—primary songwriter, bass player, and lead singer—had a fanatical interest in Alan Vega of Suicide. Ric was an adventurous listener. He produced the Bad Brains and Romeo Void and he was blown away by Alan. He brought it up to Bob that he wanted Elektra to sign Vega and let him produce the album. It was hard for Bob to turn Ric down and I was tagged to be the A&R executive.

The album, *Saturn Strip*, was electrifying. But it didn't sell well, which meant a problem for the bottom line and when the bottom line was at risk, Bob was not happy, so he dropped Vega. But before letting him go, Elektra distributed Alan's next album, *Just a Million Dreams*. Ric produced two of the tracks, and Howard Thompson, head A&R at Elektra, took over the project.

It was a real contradiction that such a misunderstood artist on the rock scene, who sometimes terrorized his audiences, became an important voice for Ocasek, one of the industry's most popular, mainstream artists. Vega once spoke of Ocasek in glowing terms: "When I work with him, I know I'm in God's hands."[1]

✿　　✿　　✿

Nine months later, I decided to sign my first band. They were a power pop group from Red Bank, New Jersey, called Shrapnel. They wore military uniforms on stage, had been on the New York scene for a few years and were regulars in the local clubs. They had put out a couple of singles that were really cool and they were managed by Legs McNeil, the co-founder of *Punk* magazine. Curiously, they were favorites of the writer Norman Mailer, who hired them to play at a number of his parties. Mailer was enticed by the punk rock movement because he "did genuinely like the music—its energy, precision, and violence."[2] I adored Shrapnel, and they were friends of mine. Also, I was anxious to start signing bands.

I ended up overseeing the recording of a five-song EP, which was produced by Richie Cordell and Glenn Kolotkin of Hall of Fame Records and FilmWorks. The remainder of the EP was produced by Vince Ely, drummer for the Psychedelic Furs. It did fairly well on the college radio circuit but they didn't make a heavy splash in sales and, eventually, Bob and the label asked me to release them from their contract. Bob never really liked them, but that wasn't the point—they weren't selling—and *that* was the point.

It was my first signing and it was a disaster—a complete failure. Thinking about it now, I know I was still very young and too eager—I had blinders on—blinded by a success that hadn't arrived yet. I was heartbroken.

Unfortunately, I had to inform the band that Elektra was letting them go. They took it as best as they could. I couldn't try and make things better for them in other ways, I had to keep moving forward.

16

GAME CHANGER

One day, while I was handling the onslaught of phone calls from agents and lawyers and trying to listen to the hundreds of demo cassettes burying my desk, I got a call from a man named Jon Zazula (a.k.a. Jonny Z). He ran an independent record label located in Old Bridge, New Jersey, which he and his wife, Marsha, started in 1982. It was called Megaforce and they had signed a number of heavy metal bands.

Jonny Z had contacted me because he knew I was interested in the kind of music he was promoting. He was looking for a big company to distribute his artists' albums and fund his label.

Jonny was a big, bushy man with curly brown hair and dark eyes, and every time I saw him, he was dressed in black with scuffed cowboy boots. He was very smart and fiercely loyal to his artists. He wanted to make success happen for all of them but particularly for a band called Raven. He pushed the UK metal band on me because he said they were his darlings, and he was sure they would be huge. There were also two other acts on the Megaforce label: Anthrax and Metallica.

We became friendly and after our third meeting, he asked me if Elektra would fund a demo in hopes that Raven would get signed to the label. So,

I came back with a check for $5,000 and told him, "Let's do this—I want to hear five of Raven's best songs. Get it back to me as soon as you can."

He returned to New Jersey and oversaw Raven's recording, while I listened to the other artists on his label. One of the first albums Megaforce had released was *Kill 'em All* by Metallica. I knew about Metallica when Phil Caivano and I went to see them at L'Amour in late 1982. There was also a cassette of Metallica demos going around the metal underground that eventually made its way onto my desk. Everything I had seen and heard by them, up to that point, completely blew me away.

I looked through the box of albums from Megaforce which Jonny had sent to my office. I pulled out *Kill 'em All*, and threw it on the turntable. A convergence of major events began happening right in front of me.

After the first few seconds, I fell off my chair. The sound fuckin' destroyed me. Although I had seen them live and heard the demo tape, I wasn't prepared for what I was hearing right then on their debut album.

I listened to the song "Hit the Lights," then I put on "The Four Horsemen" and turned up the volume. I completely lost my shit. What I heard right then—was a game changer.

It wasn't just loud and aggressive, it had elements of British heavy metal, punk rock, and classic rock, but more than anything it had speed. Real, fuckin' speed. On top of that, the songwriting was extremely strong. I couldn't believe how precise the musicianship was at that speed either. It was groundbreaking.

I quickly realized that I had to move into stealth mode. I learned that Metallica was doing a show at The Stone in San Francisco, so I quietly planned a business trip out there. I told Bob there were some new artists playing that sounded rather promising.

It was to be a fast, undercover mission. When I got to The Stone a few nights later, I grabbed a drink and sat down. Metallica came out onto the stage, and I watched them bang out "Whiplash" and "Phantom Lord." It was absolutely soul crushing. What I saw was exactly what I heard back in my office. I knew that was it—I had to get this band signed to Elektra.

After the show, I went backstage, and said, "Hi! I'm Michael Alago. I work for Elektra Records."

Lars walked over to me and said hello. Turns out, he was the point person.

"I think you guys are incredible!" I gave him my business card which he took and looked at very closely.

"When you are in New York next, please give me a call," I said. "I'll bring everybody from the company to come see you."

✻   ✻   ✻

I flew back to New York and I kept myself out of sight. I didn't tell Bob I had gone to see Metallica, and I certainly didn't tell Jonny Z. The main reason I kept it quiet from Bob and the rest of Elektra was that I was essentially interfering with someone else's record contract, namely Metallica's with Megaforce. That was a serious problem. Even though we hadn't made an offer yet or contacted business affairs about a possible signing, I felt inside my bones—I would get Metallica, one way or another.

A few months later, the phone rang in my office:

"Hi, its Lars Ulrich."

"Hey, Lars! How are you?"

"Good! We haven't heard from you since The Stone, but I wanted to let you know we're coming to New York, and we're going to be part of a three-act bill at Roseland—a Megaforce evening, with Raven and Anthrax, and we're in the middle slot."

Gotcha!

17

METALLICA

That night, in 1984, as my friends and I arrived at Roseland and quickly made our way to the bar, I knew I was in for something earth-shattering. We ordered a few beers and met up with Bob Krasnow and Mike Bone,[1] vice-president of promotion at Elektra. I had asked them to come and see Metallica with me, because I knew I would ultimately need Bob's approval in order to get them signed.

Bob and Mike both hung out at the bar during the show, while I pushed my way into the crowd and eventually lost my friends.

The place was packed. There must have been over 3,000 fans—all of them screaming, head-banging, and raising their fists in the air. There was an intense electricity everywhere. The place reeked of beer and most of the crowd was made up of sexy young men in jeans and black leather jackets. They all knew they were about to hear something that would completely blow their fuckin' heads off.

When Metallica finally hit the stage, the crowd went ballistic. Although Anthrax had played a raucous first set and got a terrific reception, ultimately, the crowd wasn't there for them. They weren't there for Raven either. The crowd was waiting for Metallica to come on and destroy the place.

At the start of the show, they smashed into the pounding lead of "Phantom Lord" with speed and brutal force, followed by "The Four Horsemen," then the debut of the song "For Whom the Bell Tolls." The sound was loud, raw, and crushing. The music was more intricate than I'd ever heard before—it broke down everything any of us knew about metal.

In the early eighties, Thrash Metal was still a slowly simmering scene. Not unlike the punk rock world six years previously, these types of metal bands were boiling under the radar—though it wouldn't be long before they became the radar themselves, the standard against which everything else in that genre would be judged.

When the show ended, the crowd was still insane, screaming madly, banging into each other, crushing and stomping on the balcony, I thought the ceiling rafters would crash down on us. The fans were all grabbing one another's leather jackets, in awe and disbelief. We never wanted Metallica to leave the stage.

After the set, I ran to the backstage area. Muscled, tattooed, security guards wandered around with suspicious looks at everyone. My heart was pounding. Raven was gearing up to go on stage and roadies and techies dashed around, prepping for the headlining stars.

I found Metallica's dressing room and I pushed open the door, startling all of them. I remember James pulling his towel off his face and looking at me, completely confused. I quickly turned, shut the door, and locked it. Then I looked back at all of them: James Hetfield, Lars Ulrich, Cliff Burton, and Kirk Hammett. I ran up to each one and hugged and kissed them, screaming how fuckin' awesome I thought they were, how I had never heard anything like them, ever. I could see that these four young guys from the West Coast with sweat dripping down their long, curling hair, thought I was out of control. After they wiped the moisture off their faces, and looked at me, I'm sure they were thinking, "Who the fuck *is* that guy?"

Well, I certainly didn't look like a fucking record company executive. I was the same age as they were—twenty-two, twenty-three—from Brooklyn, New York, in black jeans and a Metallica T-shirt. I looked at them with excitement and said, "I'm gonna sign you and your lives are going to change forever!"

At first, it seemed like they were about to laugh until Lars suddenly announced, "Guys! That's Michael Alago from Elektra Records!"

※   ※   ※

The next day, the four of them showed up at the Elektra offices. I met them in the conference room and ordered up Chinese food and beer. Everyone was excited and anxious to talk. Cliff Burton, the dashing bass player with long, dark, reddish hair and bell bottoms with elephant-sized flared legs, was the most talkative and professional. He led the conversation as we bounced ideas and plans back and forth. They were also interested in Elektra's recording history so I gave them cassettes and LPs of the Doors, the Stooges, and the MC5. We had a terrific afternoon. There was only one problem.

They were still under contract with Megaforce.

18

A FORCE TO BE RECKONED WITH

Being in the metal community and having listened to heavy metal for years, I knew signing Metallica was going to be historic. They didn't sound like anyone else and no one sounded like them.

But I was getting in the way of a band's contractual obligations with another record company, and I knew that could cause some major problems for me, because this issue was bigger than my career—it could affect Elektra's parent company, Time Warner, and, thus, Krasnow. Except there was no way that I couldn't take that risk, and the band wanted me to sign them as well.

"Nothing is impossible," I let the guys know.

After we finished our Chinese food and drank some more beer, I called Krasnow and asked him to come into the conference room. A few minutes later, he entered in his characteristic regal way, impeccably dressed with a lit cigar in his mouth. He was the older man in the room with that overwhelming charisma dominating everyone. He nodded to the guys and shook all their hands.

"That was an incredible show at Roseland, gentleman," he winked. "Listen, Michael wants you here at Elektra, so we want you here—and we will make it work." Then he left, and we all raised our beers in ecstatic celebration.

I don't believe Bob loved Metallica, but I think he trusted me, and even more importantly, Bob knew what would sell. He just *knew*.

Meanwhile, Megaforce was still there. That issue had grown bigger than me because it was now a matter of getting the band out of an old record contract and into a new one. Bob knew about this, but he expected me to handle it. It was a scary process, but I had to make it work.

So, I called Jon Zazula. I had told him I had listened to the Raven demo and thought it was terrific but that it wasn't for us. Then I told him about our interest in signing Metallica. Well, that kind of killed the already awkward conversation. He completely blew up. He was furious.

Except, I wanted them. As James Hetfield later said, "[Megaforce was] helping a baby grow . . . at some point it's going to walk on its own, and you wave goodbye."[1]

Gary Casson in Business Affairs—for whom I had the ultimate respect—was now brought in, and the lawyers took on the battle.

Finally, Elektra granted Megaforce a healthy financial deal. Megaforce agreed. Metallica was now ours. And that was my first major lesson in the demanding record business: Money talks.

We ended up producing numerous albums for Metallica, funding and supporting their meteoric rise to world domination while they became one of the highest selling rock 'n' roll bands in history. I have remained good friends with them throughout it all as they have changed the landscape of music, of what people were listening to in hard rock and heavy metal worldwide.

✾   ✾   ✾

In 1986, Metallica went on tour in Europe to support their latest release *Master of Puppets*, which, despite almost no radio airplay or music videos, became Metallica's first certified platinum album selling over six million copies and receiving worldwide critical acclaim.² It was also the first thrash metal album to receive platinum status.

One night, on the European leg of their world tour, Metallica's bus was driving through Dourap, Sweden and it skidded on some black ice and turned over. No one was seriously harmed, except their bass player, Cliff. He was pinned under the bus. It was a surreal experience, and James went ballistic on the driver. He was sure the driver was drunk or fell asleep or something.³

> [A]ttempts were made to rescue him from underneath the bus by lifting it with a crane, but the crane slipped, and the bus crashed down on top of Burton a second time. Band members and onlookers have given different accounts of whether Burton died upon first impact or when the bus came down again, but the promising young star died at the scene.⁴

The group was devastated and seriously talked about shutting the band down. They had lost a beloved brother, a lovely young man, a magnificent musician.

After many discussions, the guys finally decided, in honor of Cliff and the unique beauty and strength he had brought to the music, to continue on.

19

THAT METAL GUY

I became *"the* metal guy" at Elektra and in the industry. During 1986, I signed Metal Church. They were a heavy metal band originally formed in San Francisco before they relocated to Aberdeen, Washington. I bonded with the guitarist and lead writer of the band, Kurdt Vanderhoof, not only because he was a brilliant songwriter but when we learned we were both gay, we connected in an even more profound way. At that time, there weren't many out, gay musicians, especially in the world of heavy metal.

I thought Metal Church was great. They had generated a lot of interest in Seattle and the metal community. Their first independent record was the self-titled *Metal Church*. They had a powerhouse vocalist named David Wayne, who was up there with Judas Priest's Rob Halford. He was a real contender. I loved working with him. Unfortunately, he passed away from complications after a car crash.

Elektra licensed and distributed their first album, then recorded their second album, produced by Mark Dodson, called *The Dark*. Their third and final release for Elektra was *Blessing in Disguise*. It featured their new vocalist, Mike Howe. They went on to record for a few other labels, and my personal favorites were their albums *The Human Factor* and *Generation Nothing*.

In 1986, I went to see Metal Church when they opened for Metallica at the Odeon in London. I was completely drunk and someone from Kerrang magazine put me in one of those shopping carts and wheeled me to the gig. While I was there, I started head banging to Metal Church and I cracked my head open. I don't remember anything that happened after that. The next thing you know, I woke up in Kurdt Vanderhoof's room and my head was stuck to the rug from all the blood that had gushed out. It was almost comical, except when I picked myself up, the scab that had developed over-night was ripped off and fresh blood spewed out all over again.

I was also interested in Flotsam & Jetsam. All of the band members then—Eric A.K., Edward Carlson, Kelly Smith, Troy Gregory—had such magnetic personalities, and Michael Gilbert, their lead guitarist, was no exception. I've always had affection for him and his killer stage presence. They had recorded one album in 1986, called *Doomsday for the Deceiver* for Metal Blade Records and I was very impressed with it. It was the only album that featured Jason Newsted. I had gone to see them at Rockers Nightclub in Phoenix, Arizona. I loved them immediately—they were part of this new breed of bands that fell under the title of "Thrash," and that was a sound I totally related to.

At this point, I had wanted to sign them, but unfortunately everything was getting a bit chaotic. There was a definite problem. Lars had asked me about a recommendation for a new bass player for Metallica and I had sug-gested Jason. That meant he would be leaving Flotsam—which he eventu-ally did. I still signed them and in late 1987, we started production on the album *No Place For Disgrace*, produced by the band and Bill Metoyer. It was ranked number four on Loudwire's "Top 10 list of Thrash Albums not released by the Big Four." [1] Although my professional relationship with Flotsam was brief, I have nothing but love and respect for their hard work ethic and the quality of music they continue to create—*Ugly Noise*, being one of my favorites, and they raised the bar last year when they released their 2019 album, *The End of Chaos*.

Later in 1986, I was asked to A&R the group Dokken. Dokken was formed in 1979 and had released a few albums through Elektra, starting in 1984. The band members were Don Dokken, Mick Brown, Jeff Pilsen, and on lead guitar, George Lynch—a charming, magnetic metal-god of a guitar player. He was revered by many other musicians throughout the world. Eventually, we also recorded a few albums with George and his band, Lynch Mob.

In early 1988, we went on tour in Japan to support Dokken's fourth album, *Back for the Attack*. We went to Tokyo, Nagoya, and Osaka. It was a full-on headlining tour and we ended up recording it live, with plans to release it as an album when the tour finished. We hired a Japanese Mobile Unit studio to do the work, but when the company I was referred to faxed me their contract, I was shocked to see how much they planned to charge Elektra. Not only were they being paid to do the recording work, they demanded an outrageous fee on top of that. I couldn't believe it, so I called them and asked them to explain themselves. Without a moment's hesitation, they said the additional cost was for "smoother communication." They were one of the top-notch recording units in Japan, and we had to use them, but they were robbing us blind.

The live album of the tour, *Beast from the East*, was released in 1988 and was nominated for the Grammy Award for Best Metal Performance in 1990.[2]

While we were doing the gigs in Japan, we had a few really drunken nights. Once, George and I went to a very popular nightclub called The Lexington Queen. We were hootin' and hollerin' and drinking up a storm. The Lexington was also a place where U.S. army guys went to party.

At some point in the night, I had my eyes fixated on some army beefcake. He did not appreciate my attention, and a brawl ensued. In trying to protect me, George got our asses thrown out of the club. We laughed uncontrollably and staggered around Tokyo, drinking more and more.

George knew that I loved the British pop band Dead or Alive. Somehow—we either walked or took a taxi—and we ended up at a gay disco on the 35th floor of a huge skyscraper. We were insanely drunk at that point and went over to the DJ, who spoke a little broken English, and asked him to play "There is Something in My House" by Dead or Alive. We jumped out onto the empty dance floor and went wild. I think we were the only ones out there.

After that, it was all a blackout to me.

20

HIV ANONYMOUS

In the middle of 1983, I moved to Washington Street, just a few blocks north of Christopher Street, in the West Village. The Hudson River, off the West Side Highway, was a short walk away. I had moved into a small studio, with a working fireplace and a bathroom with beautiful pink and black vintage tiles. Finally, I was living in a place by myself, and I loved it.

At this time, though, the waterfront was in an outrageous state of decay, rot and deterioration stretching all the way along the Hudson River down to the southern tip of Manhattan. Since the seventies the docks had been completely abandoned, with empty sheds and rusted buildings, which were true ghost towns—desolate and rat-infested.

Yet the piers became a hot spot for many emerging artists and photographers at the time. On the weekends, I would walk through the destroyed rooms and see gorgeous murals painted on the walls by Keith Haring, David Wojnarowicz, Luis Frangella, and the site-specific installation art of Gordon Matta-Clark. At that same time, historic photos were being taken by Peter Hujar, Stanley Stellar, and Al Baltrop.

The piers also became famous for anonymous sex in the gay community. The public phones along the West Side Highway were ringing off the hook and, if you answered any of the calls you were urged to come up to the anonymous caller's apartment and have nameless sex.

On the piers themselves, there were amazingly gorgeous men—all naked—lying on concrete slabs as the sun streamed through the open windows of the abandoned buildings. There were all kinds of men: daddy types, bodybuilders, young teenage guys from the suburbs, and older men from the neighborhood. They wandered around those haunted, abandoned rooms—most of the time with leather vests on, worn jock straps and work boots. Sex was going on everywhere.

There were a lot of large holes in the floors of the abandoned buildings and, because canvases were thrown over them, you had to be careful late at night not to step on them or you would fall right into the Hudson River. Many men were often pulled out of the river because, in the darkness, it was hard to avoid all the craters.

In the Meatpacking District there were trucks that delivered beef for supermarkets and stores throughout the city. At night, when the trucks were parked, many men did heavy cruising around them. They would roll up the hatch in the back of the truck and go in to have sex, then leave. It was either the piers or the trucks. Or both.

During one of the many nights when I wandered up and down West Street having drinks at the Anvil, the Eagle, or the Spike—and was thoroughly drunk and drugged up—I went to the piers with the crowds of men roaming around the forgotten water's edge. It was exciting, titillating, mysterious and, mostly, anonymous.

❊   ❊   ❊

In 1981, it was reported that a group of gay men in Los Angeles had developed a rare form of cancer called Karposi's sarcoma. It was accompanied by severe immune deficiency and there were reports about a group of people—nearly all of them gay—who had died from it.

As the months rolled into 1982, it became clear that this new virus could be spread through homosexual and heterosexual sex, as well as

IV drug use. By September 1983, the CDC named the virus AIDS, and nearly 50 percent of those diagnosed with it were dead.[1] Most of the dead were gay men and "[b]y 1985, the structures along the piers [were all] torn down as the AIDS pandemic struck and the city began to demolish areas of 'potential contagion.'"[2]

A serious fear, nearing terror, moved through all of us in the gay community. Every day, I was frozen with both shock and complete confusion.

My doctor, Barbara Starrett,[3] was aware of the new and fast-spreading disease. A test had been developed for HIV, which the National Cancer Institute found was the likely cause of AIDS[4] and Barbara wanted to test me for it.[5]

She did, and the result was positive. I must've sat with her for an hour, in tears. I had seen so many men dying around me. Thousands of fears raced through my mind. What in the world was my future? Would I survive this? And at the top of my rising panic—the main reason for my tears was—how do I tell my mother?

I kept working despite my constant feeling of imminent doom. Honestly, I was fine physically. My doctor said that, despite my diagnosis, I was asymptomatic, though that didn't calm me down much. It just meant that I could keep working, which I did—to forget, to put my mind elsewhere. I kept drinking for the same reason.

✿   ✿   ✿

I don't remember exactly when I told her, but it was probably a few months later.

"Mom, I have to tell you something."

I was sitting at her kitchen table in Borough Park, with my sister, Cheryl. She brought me a cup of tea.

"What is it?" she asked and sat down across from me.

I started coughing, trying not to break down, trying to hold myself together.

"Uh, well . . . I'm very sick, Mom."

I started to cry and so did Cheryl. Even though I hadn't said what it was yet, Cheryl had figured it out.

Mom looked at me, tears were building in her eyes.

"I have HIV." I started sobbing. Mom began tearing up. I don't think she fully understood the impact of what I was telling her. Blanche and her girlfriends were old school. She spent most of her days with them on the front stoop of our apartment building, or watching *One Life to Live*.

She knew I was gay, though I don't think it mattered to her because we never really discussed it, and I'm sure she didn't know what HIV was.

Later that day, I heard her talking to her girlfriends Joann and Sue on the phone. Maybe they explained more to her about the virus even though those ole gals got all their information from *The Six O'clock News*, which, at that time, was filled with alarm and shock about HIV and AIDS. When Mom put the phone down, I watched her breathe heavily and then she started weeping. At that moment she grabbed me and Cheryl and we fell into each other's arms, in tears. It was devastating.

Meanwhile, I had just started working at Elektra Records. I was committed to making my new job a success, while hoping that I would remain asymptomatic and as healthy as possible.

21

FAT AND FELT

I knew from a very early age that music defined who I was, but I also knew I was a visual person. That came out in many ways. One of them was when I became enthralled with the German conceptual artist, Joseph Beuys.

When I started working at Elektra, Mitchell Krasnow was working there as well, but because his focus was on international A&R, he was in Europe a lot. In 1983, Mitchell was in Berlin checking out a gothic new wave band called Belfegore; they were on the independent label Pure Freude, owned by Carmen Knoebel. Carmen was the wife of the well-known artist Imi Knoebel, a close friend of Beuys.

When he saw Belfegore live, Mitchell knew he wanted to sign them on the spot. While he was still in Germany, he saw an exhibition of Beuys' work and sent me a postcard from the show. I was captivated when I saw the image.

Joseph Beuys was a German-born artist active in Europe and the United States from the 1950s through the early 1980s, who came to be loosely associated with that era's international, proto-Conceptual art movement, Fluxus. . . Beuys is especially famous for works incorporating animal fat and felt, two common materials—one organic, the other fabricated, or industrial—that had profound personal meaning to the artist.[1]

Beuys was doing something totally different than anyone else. The fantastic story, regularly told by Joseph, was that his airplane was shot down when he was a soldier during the Crimean War, and he was rescued by Tartar tribesmen who "wrapped him in insulating layers of felt and fat to keep him from freezing to death."[2]

Fat and felt became central elements in his work. When I went to see his exhibition, *Plight*, at the Anthony d'Offay Gallery on Dering Street in London, there was a piano wrapped entirely in felt and all the walls were covered in rolls of felt, as well.

> *Plight* refers [to] a precise moment: to dampen the sounds of building work next door, Beuys has promised the gallerist a work that opposed silence to sound. The installation consists of two spaces lined with thick rolls of felt. Once inside, the visitor experiences a sense of warmth and an ambivalent sense of isolation or insulation, of being both protected and cut off from the world.[3]

While I was there, I purchased one of Beuys' exquisite books made of felt with a red cross insignia on the cover. It was entitled *Joseph Beuys and Medicine* and was really cool because it had a handle similar to a doctor's medical bag. Unfortunately, a few months later, there was a flood in the Elektra offices and the book was destroyed. I was never able to find another one.

The story about Beuys being wrapped in fat and felt after the accident during the Crimean War has been disproven. That the story was untrue is indicative of an odd undercurrent of humor in Beuys' work.

But I was completely star struck. After I got that postcard from Mitchell, I quickly started researching everything Beuys. One of the first things I did was go to the Strand Bookstore on Broadway, because I knew they had a large variety of American and European art monographs. I was sure I could find works on Beuys there, and I did: "Joseph Beuys Wasserfarben/Watercolors: 1936–1963"[4] and "Joseph Beuys: Olfarben/Oilcolors 1936–1965."[5]

I immediately fell in love. Although I wasn't thrilled with the high prices, I had to have them, so I put them on my corporate card and called it "research." I ended up collecting over fifty books on Beuys.

Meanwhile, Mitchell learned about a show that was happening called "*Von hier aus—Zwei Monate neue deutsche Kunst in Düsseldorf*"[6] and it was going to be a major event in the art world in 1984. Every leading European artist would be there, among them: Sigmar Polke, Imi Knoebel, Georg Baselitz, and, of course, the master himself—Joseph Beuys. I was filled with excitement—all I could think was how I could not miss that show. It was my chance to meet him.

The exhibition was held inside an enormous airplane hangar, and the moment we walked in, I was overtaken by all of the magnificent paintings and sculptures.

When Beuys came through the door, a hush came over the entire place—a complete silence. He just walked through, nodding to everyone. There were some people trailing him, who I believe were journalists and photographers. The first thing he did was go over to one of his works and start inspecting it. The work was made up of multiple four-foot-high pieces of felt with a rectangular plate of copper on top of each of them.

When I got a clear view of him, I just stood there, speechless. It took me a few minutes to remember to breathe. When I finally did, I said to myself, "Okay. Get yourself ready." I *had* to talk to him, but I was extremely nervous.

After Beuys spoke with some journalists, he walked around and made his way to a very long, rectangular table. I was frozen as I watched him. Carmen Knoebel then came over to me and said, "Would you like to meet Joseph?"

I could barely answer. She nudged me toward him and he stood up and extended his hand to me.

"Hello, Mr. Beuys, I think the world of you." My voice was shaking a little. "I'm here visiting from New York City . . ."

"Ah," he replied. "New York City, I know it very well! From Rene Block." At this point, I quietly took my camera out of my bag, and asked:

"May I please take a Polaroid of you?"

"Of course."

I also showed him a Polaroid that I had taken of one of his pieces and asked if he would sign it; he said yes. Then he offered:

"Would you like to sit down here with me?"

I agreed as quickly as possible then sat there for a while watching him sign posters and postcards for a long line of admirers. I don't recall how much time we were there but when he was finishing up, he looked under the table and pulled out a cardboard box. He placed it in front of me, and inside of it there were fifty postcards of all of his "actions."

"This is a gift," he said.

He then started writing on the top of the box: "For Michael. Joseph Beuys," and then he drew a picture of his world famous hat.

"This is for you." He handed the signed box to me. I was overcome with excitement by such a generous gesture. At some point in the evening, his close friends came together for some drinks. He introduced me to his wife, Eva, and we all sat around talking about the event and having a truly wonderful time. It felt like a dream.

I remained in a pure state of awe being around that gracious man and was so deeply saddened when I learned of his death, on January 23, 1986. To this day, I go to every Beuys exhibition I can find—anywhere in the world.[7]

> Every human being is an artist, a freedom being, called to participate in transforming and reshaping the conditions, thinking and structures that shape and inform our lives. [8]
>
> —Joseph Beuys

22

HUMANITY

Dureau's photographs celebrate the people of his community who are not usually given a platform of such honest regard. He acquaints us with deformity not as something "freakish" and "other" but, rather, as something natural, presenting his models with unflinching visual clarity while also rendering what resonates as truthful about them as individuals.[1]

I was a young photographer, discovering what I wanted to focus on, what would be my vision. I explored everything from flora and fauna at the Botanical Gardens, to galleries exhibiting homoerotic photography. My interests seemed pulled toward images of flowers and the nude male. I learned about that through the works of particular photographers who explored gay iconography.

In 1978, I was still living at home in Brooklyn while attending SVA. On one of my many expeditions into Manhattan, I came across some remarkable work by a photographer named Arthur Tress at a downtown gallery called the Robert Samuel Gallery. The gallery exclusively featured male erotica and it is where I was also introduced to the works of Joel Peter Witkin and early Robert Mapplethorpe.

When I saw Tress' images, I was completely fascinated. I fell in love with one particular photo of two men sleeping and it seemed like they were lightly covered with dust—the sunlight streaming across the photograph was extremely beautiful.

I always thought my last name was Rockefeller because if I wanted to purchase something bad enough, I was going to get it, no matter how broke I was. That's what happened with a photograph by Arthur Tress. I asked the gallerist how much the image was and he said $125. Although that isn't much now—in 1978, for a kid still in college and living at home, it was a small fortune.

But I bought it anyway because I had saved some money, and I made sure not to tell my mother or my sister or anybody how much it cost, because they would have thought I lost my mind.

Last year, when I was back in Portland, Oregon, I visited Ampersand Bookstore—a very hip shop that carries art and photography books. I have been there a few times over the years, and they knew I was a photography and book collector. They also knew that I only wanted to see photobooks that dealt with the male image. That day last year, the owner, Myles Haselhorst, said to me, "Do you know about Arthur Tress?"

"Of course!" I replied.

"Oh, I have something special," he said, and went to the back of the store.

I made sure not to get too excited because I knew Tress' work was very expensive. A few minutes later, he returned and showed me a triptych box with a book about Tress in the middle and two provocative photographs by him on the left and right sides. They were both signed and numbered from the years 1979–1980. I couldn't believe it.

"It's been sitting here forever—uh—how's $350?" he asked me.

My mouth dropped.

"Oh, that's perfect—just put it on the counter," I said to him, thinking to myself that each of those prints would easily go for a thousand dollars. I knew I was getting a deal and I was more than delighted.

But back in 1978, purchasing the work of Arthur Tress was the beginning of my photography collecting. Black-and-white photographs completely fascinated me and I knew, even then, that whenever I made money, I was going to make that investment—and, boy, did I ever!

Not long after I discovered Tress, I was soon introduced to the paintings and photographs of George Dureau. I was completely astonished by his compelling and provocative work, and when I went to New Orleans to meet him, and purchase some of his photography, I came across a remarkable human being, who ended up being my friend for over thirty years.

George was an enormous artistic presence in New Orleans. His work appears at landmarks throughout the city, such as a large bronze bust of Artemis in front of Harrah's New Orleans Casino overlooking Canal Street, a Dureau-painted mural depicting mythic Mardi Gras across a wall at Gallier Hall, and cast-bronze nudes on the gates of the New Orleans Museum of Art.

George considered himself a painter even more than a photographer. He had a unique and innovative approach to his subjects in photography, which spoke volumes about the humanist he was at heart.

> Dureau's framing of his models allowed the observer to see more than just nudity. Mainly, he believed it allowed the observer a chance to gauge a sense of who the model was, rather than what they were capable of sexually.[2]

George mostly photographed three types of people: amputees, dwarves, and black men. Often these people were his friends—some were homeless; some even had hustler mentalities. Many were from a group that was not easily accepted in society, but George gave them that acceptance. One never felt like he exploited the people he photographed. George expressed what the scholar Charles Summers saw as "foremost a matter of empathy."[3]

George would take on a lot of these guys as hired hands, feed them, and let them clean his house for money, though there were plenty of times he didn't let this generosity go too far.

Whenever I went to New Orleans, I would go to Tommy's Florist, get a big bouquet of Casablanca Lilies and walk over to George's home. I also did that the very first time I met him.

That day, I was walking down Dauphine Street—it had rained that morning and the street was still dark and wet. As I approached George's place, I saw a man standing outside and he kind of looked like Rasputin. He had crazy raven hair, a wild, unkempt beard and a butcher knife in his hand. He was swinging the knife in the air and yelling at a one-legged kid on crutches in front of his building.

"You cannot just show up here whenever you want!" he was screaming at the kid.

"But, Mr. George! Mr. George!" the kid cried. "My clothes are all wet!"

"That's *your* problem!"

It was right then that he saw me.

"Who are you?" he said, eyeing me. "And what do *you* want?"

Holding my flowers out, I said, "George! I'm Michael Alago!' and immediately his arms went up, butcher knife still in hand.

"Oh, my dear! Finally, we're getting to meet! Please come inside!"

The kid then wandered off. I think George gave him a few bucks to get some food.

George and I went into his house. When he closed the door, we walked upstairs to the second floor and, as we did, I noticed a brown prosthetic leg with a shoe still on it on one of the steps. I asked, "George . . . who does that belong to?"

Very casually, as he headed toward the kitchen, he said, "Oh, we had a party last night."

"Okay, uh, is that person still here?" I asked.

"No," he replied. "He wandered off somewhere in the middle of the night, but I'm sure he'll come back for his leg."

It was a circus whenever anyone visited George's home. I was totally in love with his personality. He was a beautiful, down-to-earth man, and I was head over heels for his work.

Two of George's muses were Troy Brown and BJ Robinson. George started photographing Troy in 1982, and he started working with BJ—a very handsome amputee, who also became a good friend of his—around the same time.

George shot many of the same models again and again. However, when he spoke about BJ and Troy, a very deep, personal affection and reverence for those two men came through.

[George] had a way of depicting his subjects (including amputees and dwarves) that was very frank but very evocative at the same time. . . . He did it in a way that made them seem powerful and heroic, which is not easy to do. He loved the male figure. Especially in his painting, he had a way of making his figures seem very mythological, like gods and centaurs, but at the same time it's as if they stepped right out of Carnival.[4]

He also photographed Otis Battiste and Glen Thompson many, many times over the years. George was very close with both of them and had known them for a long time. They both had a tendency to be petty thieves. When they came to clean George's loft from top to bottom to earn money, often Otis would go into George's wallet and pants pocket and help himself to a little bit of extra cash. They were kind of harmless, but I found myself starting to keep an extra eye out for George.

There was a day—sometime in 2012—when I went to George's house and saw him speaking to someone outside. I didn't recognize this person as one of his models, so I asked what was going on, because I saw George handing a check over to this guy.

As I approached, and looked carefully at the guy, he said:

"George gave me some money." I turned to George.

"George did you give some money to this guy?"

"Oh, I don't remember Michael," he said.

"Ok!" I said, I grabbed the check from the guy and ripped it in half.

"You're no longer welcome here. I know your face, remember that," I warned him.

The check had been made out for $1,000. I figured this guy was someone George had met on the street. He was like that—very generous of spirit—generous with his heart, with his time, and unfortunately, his money.

George and I went up into his studio and I saw hundreds of photographs thrown all over the floor. The place looked like a tornado had just hit. I knew right then and there I had to help him organize the place. Then when I looked closely at all the pictures, I noticed the edges appeared like they had been chewed up. I picked up a few and asked George:

"What's wrong with all the edges of the photographs?"

"Oh, the mice love the silver gelatin on the prints," he casually replied.

"George! This is your work, you can't have mice eating the gelatin on the prints!"

There were big archival boxes in the corner of the studio. So, I made George some lunch, gave him a glass of white wine, then I started going through everything on the floor. I divided all of the photos into separate boxes, marking them—Dwarves, Amputees, Black Men—until I organized everything properly. I also let the Arthur Roger Gallery know what I was doing as they had represented George for over twenty-five years. At one point, though, he thought someone had stolen his pictures and I said, "George, we've been here all day! I put everything in boxes for you. Now, the mice won't eat your prints."

George's studio was usually my first stop in New Orleans, and he always put out a wealth of food for me. Sometimes, I would go there for lunch then leave to take care of whatever business I had in New Orleans, then come back for dinner. We would eat and talk and drink, laughing until two in the morning. He also loved Nina Simone, whom I had known for a decade and with whom I had recently started working. I knew she was appearing at the New Orleans Jazz and Heritage Festival, so I mentioned to George that I could bring her to his house.

"Michael! You're really going to bring Nina Simone here?" he cried.

"Absolutely!" I insisted. "You love her and she's going to love you and your pictures too! Everybody's going to have a grand ole time!"

When I brought her to George's, we sat on the veranda outside his home. George made Crawfish Étoufée and there were bottles and bottles of white wine. George ended up giving Nina a couple of large prints of nude black men, which she absolutely adored. It was a very special day for all of us.

❊   ❊   ❊

The last time I saw George was June 3, 2013. By that time he was living at the Carrington Place of New Orleans, because he couldn't take care of himself anymore. That was the first time I saw him when he wasn't in his own home, so I knew our visit was going to be very, very different.

When I arrived at Carrington, I said to the front desk receptionist, "Hi, I'm Michael Alago, and I'm here to see Mr. Dureau."

"Oh yes, of course," the receptionist replied. "I believe his friend Katie said you were coming. He's finishing getting dressed. Do you mind waiting?"

Katie Nachod was a good friend of George's and always took excellent care of him.

I waited a few minutes before a nurse took me to see him.

He was fully shaved and in all the years that I knew him, I never saw him without a beard. His hair was in a pony tail and he was put together beautifully. I was comforted knowing this place was taking good care of him.

When I entered the room, I went up to him and I said, "Hi, George!"

"Who are you, young man?" he asked, looking at me with a puzzled expression.

"George! I'm Michael Alago from New York!"

"I know Michael Alago from New York and you are certainly not him!"

"But it is me, George!"

He looked at me, slightly annoyed.

I sat quietly with him for a few minutes, then I said, "Well, George, do you know how long you've been living here now?"

"No," he informed me. "But there's about to be a performance."

"Who's going to be performing?" I asked.

"You don't worry about it," he said. "But there's going to be a performance."

All that happened was that the other people in the Day Room started walking around, being unruly and out of control. They all had dementia. One woman kept coming over, running her hands over my head and saying that I had such nice hair. There was a table with a tic-tac-toe board on it and George wanted to play, which we did. They served lunch—if you want to call it lunch—and we ate together.

As I was leaving, he said to me, "Michael, it was very nice to see you today." I smiled back at him and thought to myself—*He remembered who I was.*

When I left the building, I sat on the curb out front, and sobbed uncontrollably. I loved George so much. Thirty years of seeing this character who was beloved by everyone in New Orleans—his mind was going and it was tragic to watch.

George was a very proud man. Over the years, he rode his bicycle from home to the farmers market and back again. He did that ride like clockwork, even if he sometimes got lost. At those times, I would go out and search for him and when I found him, I would say, "Maybe you should walk the bike home with me?"

"No, you can walk, and I will meet you back at my home." He was very independent—a brilliant, noble spirit.

He died in 2014, of advanced Alzheimer's Disease.

✿   ✿   ✿

In mid-2016, I got a call from the New Orleans Museum of Art. They wanted me to appear on a panel about George Dureau's work. It was coinciding with the publication of a comprehensive book published by Aperture on George's photography entitled *George Dureau, The Photographs*.[5]

Knowing that I wouldn't be taking a scholarly approach to George and his work, I offered my personal stories about our friendship, which included the first time I met him, finding the prosthetic leg in his studio, his delicious cooking, and when I brought Nina Simone over to visit him. It ended up being a very successful discussion because people were really interested in all the stories, the world of George the human being, and how that charged his passion in photography.

> George was born December 28, 1930, in New Orleans, and lived most of his life here. New Orleans was his spiritual as well as his physical home, and he embodied the carefree and bohemian aspects of his birthplace. He was well loved by all who knew him, and he was known by many. In addition to his amazing artistic talents, he was also a bon vivant and a raconteur par excellence. . . . He was nothing if not an egalitarian, comfortable with people from all walks of life.[6]

23

THE PERFECT MOMENT

Back in the seventies, Robert Mapplethorpe went to see George Dureau in New Orleans. It was George's work that inspired Mapplethorpe to make the visit. Robert was particularly keen on seeing George's photographs of nude black men.

My friendship with Robert started in 1983. One day, I called him and introduced myself, mentioning that I worked at Elektra Records, and I would like to make a studio visit.

"I don't do studio visits," he said to me, rather abruptly.

"Really?" I asked. I was a little put off, but it didn't matter. I never took no for an answer.

"Well," I continued. "I love your work and I want to purchase something, so can we talk about it at the studio?" He asked for my phone number and said he'd get back to me.

By that time in 1983, Mapplethorpe was very well known—his work had been shown at the Holly Solomon Gallery, the Robert Samuel Gallery, and a collection of his work had been on international tours. At the time I called him, he was showing at the Leo Castelli Gallery. I knew I was pushing it by trying to connect with him—but to me, his photographs were mind-blowing, absolutely stunning.

A couple days later, he called me back—he must've checked up on me—and he said, "Okay—when would you like to come over?"

The next day, I headed over to 24 Bond Street and brought with me the biggest bouquet of white Casablanca Lilies I could find because Map-plethorpe was famous for photographing flowers. However, I had to make sure these flowers were absolutely pristine—that they were just opening, or if they had opened, that there was no fading or any grounded tips. As nice as the bouquets were for George when I visited him, I was far more careful about the state of their presentation for Robert.

When I arrived at his building, I pressed the buzzer. After he buzzed me in, I waited for the elevator to come down from the fifth floor. When it arrived, Robert opened the door. I handed him the bouquet of lilies and they actually made him smile. I immediately felt like we were going to get along.

I was wowed at that first meeting. He didn't know me, and he was a very private guy and, like he mentioned, he didn't usually do studio visits. It was a special moment.

"So, I'm not going to pull out every single photograph for you," he announced. "Is there something specific you want?"

"Yes, I like your 'Tiger Lily' and 'Larry (man with tattoo and 3 fingers).'"

"Doable." he said. "You take the flowers. There are vases in the kitchen." Then he left, and I put the lilies in water.

When he came back, he was carrying a box filled with 16 × 20 prints. Although the images were 15 × 15, they were printed on 16 × 20 paper. He started taking them out of the box and—lo and behold—there was the tiger lily and the other one was the profile of Larry. I had worshipped both from afar, having seen them in magazines and gallery shows. He leaned them up against his work desk. I lost my breath. I was overwhelmed.

"Yes! Those are the ones!" I said.

He quoted $1,500 for each one. That was a lot, but I had just started at Elektra and had a bit of money saved, so I quickly agreed.

Unfortunately, many years later, I sold both of the pieces. I was a drug addict at that point, and, well, I needed the money. In retrospect, I have total regret for selling them.

Robert and I ended up becoming good friends. We often had lunch together, and sometimes dinner. We usually went to a restaurant in the village called Vanessa's. We'd get there around eight o'clock and, on a few occasions, after we had cocktails and ordered some dinner, Robert would pull out a vial of cocaine.

I would look at him in disbelief.

"We're going to snort coke right here?" I'd whisper.

"Yeah!" he said. "Nobody's looking!"

Then we'd both snort the coke and talk, talk, talk. We never ended up eating anything and at some point, we'd get up and head to one of the usual haunts—the Spike, the Eagle, the Anvil, or, Robert's favorite, the Mine Shaft.

I had never been to the Mine Shaft before I met Robert. He took me there for the first time and it turns out Robert was not only a regular but eventually became the official photographer for the club.

The Mine Shaft was a BDSM gay sex club and bar. It had been started in the seventies and was in a building at 835 Washington Street, which was a strange coincidence because that was only a block from my apartment at 763 Washington. I never went there because it wasn't my kind of scene. It was very hardcore.

That night when we arrived, we went upstairs. It was grimy and dark and stunk like used jockstraps in a locker room. It was crowded with hairy daddies and muscled, tattooed biker types. The dress code was strictly enforced: Motorcycle leathers, plaid shirts, black boots, Western gear, and jocks.

I was stunned. Then, after the first five minutes, Robert ditched me and went off with some friends. I just stood there at the bar, by myself, thinking "What the fuck am I going to do?" I didn't know this place, I wasn't a regular there by any means, and the situation was a little unnerving.

Suddenly, a very tall man with leather pants, cowboy boots, no shirt, and a leather mask with a zipper across the mouth, came up behind me. He spun me around, unzipped the mouthpiece and started making out heavily with me. It was shocking. But that's how that place was—raunchy and unpredictable.

✿   ✿   ✿

Mapplethorpe was definitely taken by George Dureau's work. In many important ways, he was a strong inspiration for Robert. In fact, I believe he borrowed stylistically from George. For instance, an early image of Robert taken by George in 1979 was circular, a design which Robert used not much later in a fashion campaign for the Miquel Cruz Fashion house.

However, Robert was about being famous and making the money. It was a very different vibe than Dureau's vision, which came from a more folk-art mentality.

Although I only knew Robert from 1983–1989, when he died from AIDS, we had a close connection during those few years. When I worked at the Red Parrot in 1983, Robert often showed up with twenty or so people and I always arranged to comp them all. That did not make my boss happy. But I just looked back at him and said matter-of-factly—"It's Robert Mapplethorpe!"

Being a young person in the music business as well as a photography collector, I was amazed that I was friends with Robert. I loved everything that he photographed from "Jim in Sausalito" to his flower portraits. I didn't relate to the S&M and fisting pictures, although I found them intriguing. I discovered there was a subculture in New York, where those men allowed him into their lives on a very intimate level, to photograph them.

Hanging out with Robert was definitely a very different experience than hanging out with George. When I visited George, he would arrange for us to have a huge feast of New Orleans Creole cuisine and we'd sit and talk while we drank bottle after bottle of Chardonnay. I saw Robert a lot as well, but there was a different quality in our get-togethers at lunch or dinner. We had fun, but it wasn't as much of an intimate friendship as it was with George.

Robert seemed to have rules about a lot of things, especially if you asked to view his book of contact sheets, which he rarely allowed, unless you were the subject of the photo shoot. The reason was because contact sheets reveal errors, mistakes in the lighting, or the developing process. Robert abhorred errors of any kind. He only ever wanted you to see the perfect moment.

In fact, that was a distinct difference between Robert's photography and George's. The presentation of Robert's photographs was always pristine, exquisite, flawless—almost cold. George, however, created photographs that were gritty and human—described as having an "intensely personal gravity that Mapplethorpe's more objectified models often lack."[1]

There was a bodybuilder Robert photographed of whom I was enamored: his name was Roger Koch, also known as Frank Vickers to his gay film audience. He was a hot, badass model who happened to be a bit arrogant and obnoxious, but he had a body that could stop a truck. Outrageously, Robert photographed him in high heels, fishnet stockings, and a black lace garment, which was totally unexpected. You can see the perfection and purity Robert gives these photos of this rough, driven bodybuilder. It wowed me to see how Robert chose to present him. Photographers like Jack Fritscher and Stanley Stellar photographed him as well. In certain circles he became legendary. I remember seeing postcards that were printed with Roger on them at local gay bookstores. Yet he was later quoted as saying "I have nothing good to say about Robert Mapplethorpe."[2]

Around 1987, Robert started to become very ill. For a time, he was at Deaconess Hospital in Boston, recovering. In the middle of 1988, he had a big retrospective at The Whitney Museum. When he arrived on opening night, he was using a cane and looked like a very old man. He was only forty-one years old and very weak, but he showed up at the Whitney anyway.

Once, when he was briefly at St. Vincent's Hospital in early 1988, I called him to see how he was doing. He wanted to know why I had never asked him to photograph Metallica or any other musician on Elektra.

Then, without missing a beat, he insisted, "When I get out of the hospital, I want to shoot somebody for you."

I took him at his word and sent him five songs from a new young artist named Tracy Chapman, whose first record I was then overseeing at Elektra. He was delighted to be shooting her portrait because she looked like the young black boys he had always liked to photograph.

Robert was then living in a loft on West 23rd Street, and had moved his studio there. Not long after our talk in the hospital, Tracy and I went to see him for the cover shoot of her debut album. When we arrived, I noticed how delicate and fragile Robert looked, so I offered to do the shoot another day.

"Absolutely not," he insisted.

I remember Robert sitting majestically in a dark wood Mission chair next to the camera. He was in his silk, paisley housecoat and velvet mono-grammed slippers, and he had a remote shutter button on his lap. His brother, Edward, lit the photograph. I left Tracy with them for the remainder of the day.

About a week later, I received the images at the office. They were very beautiful, very tomboy-like, but they had nothing to do with the feeling of the album.

Tracy's album was somber, meditative and graceful. Robert's pictures had none of that—nowhere near the atmosphere I needed for the front cover image.

Meanwhile, I had to bring these photographs into the marketing meeting at Elektra, and let the executives know that they weren't the images I expected. Robert was world renowned at that point. But he missed the mark with these photos. I had been working on Tracy's album for the last year and I knew what the cover should express, and Robert hadn't given us what we needed.

When I showed the photos at the meeting, I expressed my concern. Elektra's president, Hale Milgrim, and Robin Sloane, vice-president of video, wanted me taken off the project. This was a major screw up.

They wanted to give Robert a "kill" fee, which is a smaller percentage of what the photographer's payment would have been. I went into a rage.

I couldn't imagine giving Robert Mapplethorpe a kill fee of any kind. I marched right into Krasnow's office.

"We absolutely cannot give Robert Mapplethorpe a kill fee!" I stated emphatically. "If you have to take it out of my Metallica royalties, then do it! We have to give him his full five figures or this will turn into a major story!"

I knew Bob didn't want that kind of press.

We ended up giving Robert the full fee even though we didn't use the photographs. I didn't get fired from the project either and then, in my own charming way, I said, "Well, I have another idea."

I had seen an illustration in *Time* magazine; it was of an angry little boy in Ireland and it was photographed by Matt Mahurin. I called Matt about doing some work for us, then sent him the songs. A few weeks later he got back to me with the idea for that now-classic image of Tracy for the album cover.

Tracy's album came out in April of 1988. A year later, on March 9, 1989, Robert Mapplethorpe died.

☼ ☼ ☼

Twenty years later, in 2009, on the anniversary of his death, I decided to visit Robert's grave. I had never visited it before and I felt it was time. That morning I called his brother, Edward.

"Hey Edward, it's Michael, you do realize it's the twentieth anniversary of your brother's death?"

"Yes," he said.

"Well, I'm going to the cemetery. I'm feeling like I have to go."

There was a brief silence before he said, "Well, hold that thought for a minute, because I think Patti was talking about going."

When I heard "Patti," my heart fluttered.

I kept myself composed and said, "Well, I am gonna go whether you guys come or not, so please let me know."

Not much later, he called me back.

"I just got off the phone with Patti," he said. "She's calling Lenny and he's going to pick us all up at Patti's house."

I took a deep breath. The day was beginning to feel very spiritual to me. Although I had been periodically in touch with Patti over the years—I hadn't seen her since I was ill with AIDS in the early nineties.

"So, where do you want to meet . . . ?" I asked.

"Patti said to come to her house," Edward replied.

I thought—perfect!

A little while later, I got to Patti's. I had brought purple tulips for her and for Robert's grave. I rang the doorbell, and her assistant, Andi Ostrowe, answered. Andi had been with Patti for many years, and I felt like she never took me seriously.

When she opened the door, she eyed me up and down.

"What are *you* doing here?"

"Um, I'm going to the cemetery with Patti and Lenny."

"Does Patti know?" she asked.

"Yes, of course, Andi," I said to her. "I don't go anywhere where I'm not expected."

"Well, okay then, wait here."

When Patti found out I was at the door, Andi invited me in and Patti screamed down from upstairs, "Michael, go up to the second floor to my studio!" As I walked up there, I felt like I was in heaven.

"I would invite you up to the third floor! But it's such a mess! Be assured though, your Maria Callas box set is next to my bed!"

"Fabulous!" I shouted back. "I'm thrilled that I'm near your bed!"

Andi left me alone on the second-floor studio and I looked around in a slow, moving, dream state. On the walls were Patti's images that she had taken with her Land 250 Polaroid camera. It looked like the beginning of a future exhibition. There were also drawings on the wall. I was in awe seeing all this work that had yet to been seen by anyone else.

After a few minutes, she came down and we hugged. At that very moment, Edward and Lenny showed up. We climbed into Lenny's car and headed out to St. John's Cemetery in Middle Village, Queens. It's was a dreary Monday. I think we were all feeling kind of awkward and somber. I don't remember there being a lot of talk in the car.

When we arrived, we checked around the cemetery, and finally found the headstone. It actually read "Maxey" which was Robert's mother's maiden name, and underneath, it read "Mapplethorpe." Both his parents were buried there with him.

We looked around for a few minutes, then we started talking about Robert, and everyone took out their cameras. We all started taking photographs, then suddenly, Patti said, "What are we, the fucking *paparazzi* here?"

That broke the tension and we all laughed.

When we knew it was time to leave, we left Patti at the graveside, by herself. Prior to that day, I don't know if she had ever visited the grave alone.

After we left, we decided, in Robert's memory, to go to a local diner and have chicken soup and grilled cheese, because those were his favorites.

24

ROLLING THE DICE

At the end of 1988, I left Elektra. It was an issue of money. I felt I should've been earning a lot more, but Bob disagreed.

I wound up at UNI Records, which was a label started by MCA in 1966, but had been closed down by 1972. Then, in 1988, a few senior executives at MCA decided they wanted to revive the UNI label and make it into a niche record company.

Although I was intrigued and fired up to do something great with UNI—I never felt completely comfortable there.

The first band I signed was Swans. Swans was a much respected, experimental rock band from New York who were absolutely brutal. The band was formed by Michael Gira, their singer and principal songwriter.

Over the years their music continued to evolve, but it still had that savage beauty at its core. By the time I got involved with them, I felt like I was in church when I listened to their majestic, hypnotic, and transcendent sound.

Swans had become very popular on the college circuit. Their rebellious lyrics were sometimes shouted, almost chanted, although Michael had a strong baritone vocal sound that came out in other songs. Attending a Swans performance, you could be assured it would be the loudest experience of your concert life. When other bands turned it up to 10, Swans usually turned it up to 12. They did this for at least two hours at every performance.

Because of their rising popularity, I became interested in them and offered them a record deal with UNI. We ended up recording the album with producer/bass player Bill Laswell from the band Material. It turned out to be extremely different than anything Swans had recorded before.

The album was called *The Burning World*—a moody, somewhat bleak, and arresting record. It was a seismic shift from what Swans previously did and were known for. The band was in agreement to record this subdued, understated record and I had a very large influence on the direction of how I heard *The Burning World* being recorded. Michael and the band agreed to do a cover of Blind Faith's "Can't Find My Way Home," which I thought worked very well within the context of the other nine songs.

I then presented the band with the image of a delicious yellow Calla Lily by Mapplethorpe, which I felt reflected the overall tone of the recording and would be perfect for the front cover of the vinyl record and the CD.

> Elegant, surprisingly tender . . . *Burning World* redefines all its precedents in The Swans Discography. Earlier celebrations of mutilation and anguish, too disturbing, too hopeless to endure at length, now suggest that only by passing through so many frames of darkness could the Swans approach pure light.[1]

Many years later, I look upon *The Burning World* as somewhat of a personal success. Nonetheless, Gira had always been very specific about Swans and in the end, he wasn't happy about the record at all. I think he felt he was being bullied by both the producer, Bill Laswell (a force of nature himself) and me. Michael wasn't pleased with the way his voice was recorded and the overall feeling of the production. I think he felt like he was not in control and that was very uncomfortable for him.

In my opinion, *The Burning World* is a small masterpiece. But when it was released, UNI did not do a lot to promote it. I think they were getting pressure from the powers-that-be at MCA—who were not feeling the vibe of the UNI label after all.

The record did well on the college radio charts because of the previous history of Swans, and reviews of *The Burning World* were mostly terrific. However, the album did not perform well overall and Swans were dropped. MCA then closed the UNI label and Michael went on to start his own, Young God Records.

While *The Burning World* was out of print, it continued to generate a lot of interest, so in 2000, a small independent label called No Limits Records picked it up and redistributed it.

> *The Burning World* is a blueprint for what Swans did later. By the end of the '90s, that album made sense. At the time, people were like, "What the hell were they doing?" But as much as Michael might hate it, it's the root of what they subsequently did.[2]

※   ※   ※

After the demise of UNI, I ended up at Geffen Records. Geffen had originally interviewed me back in 1983 but now, after six years at Elektra and two years at UNI, I think they recognized me as a sought-after A&R executive. They offered me a job in their satellite office in New York City.

The first band that was brought to me was by my dear friend, songwriter and producer Daniel Rey. He was scouting a lot of New York's East Village bands and had been working with Circus of Power and Raging Slab as well as White Zombie, whom he particularly liked. He had shopped all these bands around and ended up getting Circus and Raging signed to RCA but had no success with White Zombie. So he called me and suggested I go see them live.

I went over to a little, dingy bar on Lafayette Street under a restaurant called Indochine. The space was open for musicians to play there, though it was just a dank, dark box. When I got there, White Zombie was playing on a small stage in the farthest corner of the room. It was very, very loud. I don't remember any real songs but I liked the noise radiating from the stage, and their lead singer, Rob Zombie, exuded real charisma.

Rob had all of these dreadlocks flying everywhere and I loved all the sweat pouring off of him. After the show, I chatted with them and I thought they were the loveliest people I had ever met. Then I spoke to Rob, and we took an instant liking to each other. He said to me: "I think we're going to be big, and I'm going to direct movies, so take a chance on us." I believed him.

"Let's do some demos before we do the deal," I said.

There was a producer I was interested in named Jim Thirlwell, who was a bit of a character. He was an artist who created a lot of inventive noise, and he went under the name "Foetus." Most of the records he recorded at the time used the word "Foetus" in it: "You've Got Foetus on Your Breath," "Foetus Uber Alles," "Foetus Under Glass." I thought he was a very cool guy and that he was perfect to record the White Zombie demos.

He produced the demos for Geffen, and we loved them. Unfortunately, though, egos collided, and as a result of that, Jim did not wind up producing the album.

We ended up hiring Andy Wallace, because we loved his production work on Slayer's *Seasons in the Abyss*. While we were getting ready to record, Rob got the idea to try and get Vincent Price to appear on their debut album, because we loved his spoken word on Michael Jackson's *Thriller*.

The person who contacted Price for us was Toni Quirk. Toni was one of the best things to happen to me at Geffen when I hired her to be my executive assistant. She was super smart and literally dropped down from heaven.

Toni took the helm to contact Price and was relentless with his manager to get him to agree to be on the album, but he kept saying no. Then one day after her thirtieth phone call to his manager, Vincent Price called Toni himself:

"I decided to call you myself because you are so persistent. I just can't do it because I had such a bad experience on *Thriller* that I decided after that I would never do anything like it again."

Toni assured him the experience with White Zombie would be very different and, finally, Price agreed. Unfortunately, he was suffering from emphysema and Parkinson's disease, and was never able to make the recording.

Rob brought in another one of his outrageous ideas and that was to contact Charles Manson. So, Toni called Corcoran State Prison where Manson was incarcerated. She somehow maneuvered to get a note passed to Manson to see if he would allow his voice on the White Zombie album. She said she was so scared when she made the call, she gave a phony name. Manson never answered the note.

The band also wanted to use a sample from underground filmmaker, Russ Meyer's 1965 movie *Faster, Pussycat! Kill! Kill!* The line in the movie was "Get up and kill!" I called Mr. Meyer at his home office one morning to see if this was possible. He asked me who I was and why I was calling him, because he was sitting there with a double hernia and did not want to be bothered. I was taken aback but I let him know that I worked for Geffen Records, and that I had signed a new band who wanted to use the sample that I mentioned in my fax. Upon saying yes, he said he wanted to get paid immediately. The fee was $1,000. I faxed him a simple one-page financial document for the use. He signed it, returned it immediately, and was paid within seventy-two hours.

When the album, which was titled *La Sexorcisto: Devil Music Volume One*, was released, everyone was really excited. There was a buzz in the underground hard rock community about White Zombie, so Geffen expected massive sales.

But a few months later, it stalled. It hadn't gotten anywhere near the million mark we had expected.

Then two cartoon characters on MTV, Beavis and Butt-Head—socially inept teenage delinquents—decided White Zombie was their favorite band. Mike Judge, their creator, ended up playing White Zombie's first single "Thunder Kiss '65," morning, noon, and night. In 1993, Beavis and Butt-Head were huge, as was MTV, and within a very short time, they catapulted *La Sexorcisto* to a million units in sales.

Eventually, White Zombie recorded one more album for Geffen called *Astro Creep 2000*. However, between Rob's overwhelming ego and his desire to go solo, he ended up breaking up the band.

✿   ✿   ✿

One day, when I was at Geffen in Los Angeles, I was called up to David's office and he said to me:

"Call Bill Graham."

"Do you know what it's about?" I asked him.

"No. Call Bill Graham!"

I went to the conference room and I called him.

"Is Mr. Graham available?" I asked the person who answered the phone.

"Is this Michael Alago?"

"Uh, yes," I said.

"It's Toni! Toni Isabella!

"Oh, hi, Toni!" I said.

"Hi! Bill wants to speak to you," and she transferred the call to his office.

"Hi, Mr. Graham—?"

"*Bill*," he insisted.

I swallowed hard, feeling like I couldn't be that familiar on our first phone call, so I just said: "Good Morning! What's happening?"

"Can you come to Jacksonville over the weekend?"

"Ooooh—I'm finishing up a project right now, but I'd be happy to do that on Monday or Tuesday of next week."

"Okay, call my office and let me know what day works for you. I'll pick you up at the airport in Jacksonville. I want you to hear some music."

"Cool! Would you like to tell me who it is?"

"No." he replied.

"Okay," I said, feeling a little weird, but I wasn't about to argue with Bill Graham.

The following week, I flew to Jacksonville, and Bill Graham picked me up at the airport with his chauffeur. They were both sitting in the front seat, and I was in the back. Bill turned to me and without any prompting, started talking to me about Jimmy Page and Janis Joplin—amazing stories—pearls coming out of his mouth that were awe-inspiring. I just sat there listening and thinking to myself, "Bill Graham picked me up at the airport and I'm sitting in the car with him and his chauffeur and he's regaling me with these stories." I loved it!

We finally got to a location outside the city, and it turned out to be an empty shopping mall. I was thinking as I looked at that desolate place: "This is so *Night of the Living Dead!*"

We went into the building and all the lights were on, but it felt very strange because it appeared as if it had been vacant for some time. All of the store fronts were empty and boarded up. Scattered around the place were large green plastic plants with water fountains gushing out from the middle of each one.

We started walking down the hall. Suddenly, I was hearing music in the distance and I thought: "Wait a minute—there are some artists who are so recognizable that when you hear the first few chords of a song, you absolutely know who it is. What I heard could only be the Allman Brothers or Lynyrd Skynyrd.

We got to the end of the hall and opened the door from where I heard the music playing and there they were—*Lynyrd Skynyrd*! I was immediately transported back to a starstruck, music-loving, fourteen-year-old in Brooklyn.

As I entered the room, I was greeted by Gary Rossington, lead guitarist and founding member of the band. He approached me and said, "Hey Michael, great to have you here, but we need five minutes."

"Absolutely!" I said. Then, Artimus Pyle, their drummer, came out of the rehearsal space. He welcomed me and offered me a beer. Then he asked, "Would you like to see my scrapbook?"

"Sure!" I said.

We opened it and the first picture was of Artimus in the hospital after the plane crash with his leg up in a brace and hundreds of pins in it.

[I]n 1977 . . . during a flight from Greenville, South Carolina, to Baton Rouge, Louisiana, Lynyrd Skynyrd's tour plane crashed in a heavily wooded area of southeastern Mississippi during a failed emergency landing attempt, killing band-members Ronnie Van Zant, Steve Gaines, and Cassie Gaines, as well as the band's assistant road manager and the plane's pilot and co-pilot. Twenty others survived the crash.[3]

The entire scrapbook was made up of clippings from the plane crash; it was heartbreaking. I was very respectful while he showed it to me and said how grateful I was for those in the band who had survived, and that I could never imagine how overwhelming that experience had been for them.

It had been nearly fifteen years since the crash when their brothers were killed, and it was still at the forefront of their lives—it was *the* tie that forever bonded them.

After the accident, Johnny Van Zant took over on lead vocals. His voice blended with the band perfectly, and it was equally as badass as his brother Ronnie's.

Upon entering the rehearsal room, I introduced myself to everybody. Johnny handed me a CD of their new demos and said, "We would love to be on Geffen Records and we're now going to play you some of the songs."

So there I was standing in the room—a teenager all over again—with Skynyrd performing only for me—it blew me the fuck away.

When the songs ended, I thanked the entire band. Gary invited me to dinner later that evening, and then they asked me if there was anything else I would like them to play.

"Hell, yeah!" I said.

They started counting down and the next thing I knew they were playing "Free Bird." Not expecting them to play that, I raised my hand into the air and shouted: "Wait a minute, guys!"

They looked at me with disbelief. *No one* had probably ever told them not to play "Free Bird."

"Can you just play "That Smell?""

They looked at me again. Gary did the countdown, and they went right into "That Smell"—my favorite song. I was now sitting on the floor, like a kid, in front of Billy Powell's Hammond B3 and like I said, when you hear that very specific sound from the Hammond B3, it could only be the Allman Brothers or Lynyrd Skynyrd.

We didn't end up signing them because they just weren't the right fit for the Geffen roster at that time, but Atlantic Records picked them up for their next two album releases, *Lynyrd Skynyrd 1991* and *The Last Rebel*.

❊   ❊   ❊

I signed another artist to Geffen: Kane Roberts. He had been Alice Cooper's lead guitarist. He was a big, attractive guy, who was very talented, and he knew a lot about writing catchy rock tunes. I had seen him live with Alice, and I knew about his work on MCA. He totally impressed me.

Right away, it was clear that we got along musically and that we had a similar sense of humor. I knew I wanted to make a commercial, hard rock top-forty record with him.

I contacted the hottest producer of the day, Desmond Child, to come work on Kane's Geffen debut album, *Saints And Sinners*. Desmond was hot off the heels of Cher, Ricky Martin and Bon Jovi, among others. He was intensely busy but he wanted to make this album with Kane. However, he left it largely in the hands of his engineer, Sir Arthur Payson. At one point, Kane and I discussed the problem of Desmond rarely being in the studio, because it started to bother us.

Ultimately, though, we realized the songs were there, so we figured, let's just move forward. We also decided to pull a song off of Cher's album *Heart of Stone*, because we loved it so much. The song was called "Does Anybody Really Fall in Love?" and had been written by Jon Bon Jovi, Richie Sambora, and Diane Warren—who, at the time, could do no wrong. Every song Diane wrote turned into gold. We recorded it, and it eventually became a semi-hit for Kane, peaking at #38 on the Billboard charts.

I was doing my best to keep the vibe of the record alive in the California Geffen offices, but they were not feeling it. At some point they stopped promoting the album, and Kane was dropped. Fast forward to 2018: I executive produced the new Kane Roberts Album, *The New Normal* on Frontiers Records, which was released in 2019.

Given everything that had happened at Geffen in the early nineties, though, I was very proud that I was able to sign two remarkable artists to the label during this first stint at Geffen. I wasn't a happy camper working in the New York satellite office, though, so I left. I felt like I wanted to go home so I called Krasnow at Elektra and asked if I could come back. He was very gracious and welcoming and said, "Of course."

25

HAZELDEN

In 1992, my dad was taken to the hospital for carotid arteries in his neck. He had been smoking Kent cigarettes and eating only fried food for most of his life, so it wasn't surprising he needed an operation. A few days after they operated, he went home, but he wasn't there for long. He developed a brain aneurism and had to return to the hospital within a week.

I had a pretty short visit with him that second time, because what I really wanted, what I *needed*—was money. I told my dad that I was behind in my rent and begged him to help me out. Except that was a lie. He handed over his credit cards, I gave him a kiss, ran out the door, got cash advances from all the cards and bought more crack-cocaine.

Three days after that visit, my father died at the age of fifty-eight. I was destroyed. When I left the hospital and got on the subway I looked around and said to myself: "These people can't be going to work—my dad just died." Although my relationship with him was nowhere near as close as I had with my mom, I wish it had been more. Whenever I look at photographs of my dad as a young man in the Air Force, I see that I have his exact skin color, and his smile—we look like twins. Even my laugh is deep and intense, just like his was. He was a good man and, unfortunately, because of my drinking and drugging, I never attempted to be close with him, a reality that brings me serious regret.

Eight months later, I was in Hazelden Rehab Center in Minneapolis. When I returned home, I realized I still had the credit cards my dad had given me. I decided to cut them up. Then I wrote a letter to him and went to his grave to pay my respects and apologize. I brought a flowering plant with me and read the letter to him. I told him how sorry I was for what I did. I dug a hole in front of the headstone, cut up the cards, folded the letter, put them all in an envelope, and placed them in the hole. I covered it with soil and put the flowering plant on top. I had told him in the letter that I had been drinking and doing drugs when I took the credit cards from him, but he would be pleased to know I had gone into rehab and was getting the help I needed.

✿   ✿   ✿

Before I made it to Hazelden, I went to Liza Minnelli's apartment for a Christmas party. I had met Liza when Elektra signed her best friend, pianist Michael Feinstein. She and I hit it off immediately.

Her home was on East 69th Street. It was a stunning apartment—a real showstopper. When you entered, you were greeted by four larger-than-life-sized Warhol paintings of Liza, and in the dining room there was an equally gorgeous Warhol triptych of her mother, Judy Garland.

I handed Liza a big bouquet of white Casablanca Lilies (clearly, I had a thing for lilies) and she was overjoyed.

"Why did you come alone?" she asked.

I just shrugged, so she marched me over to a sofa in the sitting room, right next to Madonna.

"Introduce yourselves," Liza commanded with a big, radiant smile, then dashed back to the front door.

Madonna looked at me and we shook hands as I sat down next to her. It had been a long time since I had booked her at the Red Parrot, so we were kind of meeting for the first time.

We started talking about movies, specifically the one she was in the middle of making with James Russo, directed by the infamous Abel Ferrara, called *Dangerous Game* (a.k.a. *Snake Eyes*). We also talked about all the art covering Liza's walls.

We watched the many guests entering her apartment, dishing each one as they arrived. We first saw Lucie Arnaz come in with her two boys. They were pretty young, maybe ten and eleven, and one of them was so excited to see Madonna that he furiously tugged at his mother's coat. Madonna called the kid over and planted a big kiss right on his lips. I was sure he was going to piss in his pants, or faint. He just stared back at us in shock.

More guests came in. Madonna and I continued our rather camp scrutiny of the mostly "B-listers" as they arrived. Until Tony Bennett came in— definitely *not* a B-lister. Then O. J. Simpson and his wife, Nicole, showed up. Everyone went into the living room while Michael Feinstein played the piano. We all sat there for about two hours and had a few drinks, when James came over to Madonna and told her it was time to go—they had an early call the next morning.

At some point, I started to wander around the apartment. I stared at the Warhols of Liza, near the entranceway. Then, I saw her Oscar for *Cabaret* on a shelf. I reached over and lifted it with one hand. Suddenly, I had to grab it with both hands because it weighed a ton. I didn't expect it to be so heavy. The floors were pure white marble and if I dropped it, that would be a major disaster! I quickly pushed the statue back into its place and took a deep breath.

My need to drink was growing strong. I wanted something harder than white wine and champagne, which was all that was being served. The party was fabulous, yet my need for booze was overwhelming. I didn't want to make a scene, so I quietly left.

I hailed a taxi down to Times Square, to two of my favorite hustler bars— Stella's and Cats, and scored some crack. I then raced over to Club USA to see Marky Mark. I was super fired up from all the coke and after his performance, I went backstage to see him. He recognized me because he was at The Ritz the night before, and we had playfully argued about whether it would be he or Metallica who would take the next #1 album spot on the Billboard charts.

Then I pulled up his shirt and asked him to roll his stomach muscles up and down. I had seen him do that before and I loved every moment of it. I now figured I could touch his muscled abs, so I did, even though there were a few big, black security guards working for Mark hovering behind me. But Mark signaled to them that I was harmless.

It was around 3 a.m. when I went home. I was feeling frantic for some more crack. I found my crack pipe and I scraped and scraped it and then all of a sudden, my mind went into a full-blown frenzy.

I thought it was the end of the world
I felt like I was writing a book.
I thought I was going to die.

Ranting and raving, I grabbed a cab on 7th Avenue and went to my friend Carol Friedman's home in Soho. When the cab arrived, I madly rang her bell, frantically pressing the button—I was so high. Finally, she appeared at the upstairs window and threw down the keys. Many of the buildings in Soho didn't have buzzers at that time.

I ran up to her apartment and when she opened the door, I rushed in and whirled around like a crazed maniac—laughing and cackling. All I had on were a pair of boxers and an old man's winter coat with two beers in the pockets. I immediately threw off the coat and started doing push-ups—1–2–3—then I got up and grabbled Carol in my arms and twirled her around and around.

"Michael! What's going on?" she shouted.

"I'm high on CRACK!" I yelled back—the word fired me up. I laughed and kept twirling.

Turned out, of all my close friends, Carol was the only one who didn't know I was a major drug addict. I put her down on the floor and started howling, like I was in pain. Tears gushed out of me. I started crying and screaming.

"Carol! You have to help me! You have to help me!" I was so out of it—and overwhelmed with terror.

Carol was completely thrown and didn't know what to do, but she told me later, that at that very moment, she had a vision of the EMS paramedics carrying my dead body out on a stretcher. She said that when she had that vision she knew she had to do something, and fast.

"I'm taking you to the hospital," she said.

"Fine! Fine! Whatever you need to do!"

"And I'm going to tell Krasnow."

"Fine! Just help me, Carol!"

She rushed me to St. Vincent's emergency room and they immediately asked her what was wrong.

"He's high on crack," she told them.

They quickly took me to the back to see a doctor. They strapped me down on a gurney because I was so crazed and out of control. I kept screaming because I was feeling trapped. Apparently, Carol heard my screams and tried to get back to me, but the hospital staff wouldn't let her.

She then went back home and called Krasnow. She had been the creative director of Elektra Entertainment until a few years previously, but continued doing freelance work for the company, as a photographer. Bob knew her well.

Carol called him at 6:30 a.m. and woke him up.

"Bob?" she said. "Michael has to go to Hazelden."

"Why?" Bob asked.

"For drugs."

"What kind of drugs?"

"It's crack," she told him.

"Oh, for God's sake!"

Bob ended up calling Maryann at Elektra. She handled all the administrative and human resource matters and there had been a number of executives at the company who had recently gone to rehab. Unfortunately, that was the music business.

At St. Vincent's, the doctors did a complete work-up—EKG, CAT Scan, blood tests, and I eventually fell asleep. I woke up around seven the next morning and was discharged.

As I was walking down the street, I ran into Carol, who had been heading over to the hospital to get me. I smiled when I saw her.

"Where are you going?" she asked me.

"I'm heading over to Vince's in the East Village."

"No, you're not," she said.

She knew I was going to cop some more crack.

"We're going to your apartment," she said firmly.

By that time, Maryann had taken care of the paperwork to get me into Hazelden. A private car was going to pick me up the next morning to take me to the airport.

"I'm staying with you tonight, Michael—until the car comes," Carol insisted, and she slept on my couch that night. That was December 22, 1992.

✿   ✿   ✿

On the flight the next morning, a hip Jewish mom with dyed blonde hair and an exhausted look on her face sat down across from me with her fifteen-year-old son. The boy was lost in his Walkman and I could swear I heard Metallica blasting out of his headphones.

The woman's name was Ruth, and her son's was Rich. He was an adorable, husky teenager who had one of those spikey haircuts that all the kids had at the time, and was listening to everything heavy metal. I struck up a conversation with him and at some point, he told me he wanted to be an orthodontist when he grew up.

Once we landed in Minnesota and headed toward ground transportation, a man from Hazelden arrived to take me to the center, which was about an hour north from the airport. It was at that moment when I realized he was there to pick up Ruth and Rich, as well. As it happens, they were visiting Rich's dad. On the drive out to Hazelden, I continued talking with Rich and started feeling a little paternal toward him. He had a big chip on his shoulder about going to Hazelden because this wasn't the first time they were visiting his father there. Rich felt having to go on these trips just ruined Hanukkah for he and his mom. Over the next few days I often saw Ruth, Rich, and his dad on the grounds of the center.

✵   ✵   ✵

Dear Carol:

I don't know where else to start this letter except to say thanks for being a true, true friend. I love you for helping me get over the biggest obstacle in my life. Now, onto more important things. We have to discuss the significance and importance of Frankie Valli and the Four Seasons in pop music. I was just listening to the oldie stations here and "Can't Take My Eyes Off You" came on. Well! When that chorus begins and Frankie's voice is heard—if that's not a precursor to a pop anthem that changed the world, I don't know what is! I think we need the Greatest Hits CD. On another legendary note, Down to Zero CD by Joan Armatrading—a startling, uplifting, glorious record. My friend Aaron has a few songs taped on a mix cassette of songs. I forgot how wonderful this record is. A classic! When I get home, I'd like to get the CD. Also, Pirates by Rickie Lee Jones—my all-time favorite record. If all this music doesn't have your head spinning, I just want to let you know that I think Minnesota is just grand. So I think I'll stay.

Just Kidding!

I'll be here until the 20th of January—another 15 days. Do you believe I'm up and ready to rock at 6:30 a.m.? It's like the fucking army. Meditation. Breakfast. Lecture. Process (Discussion about Lecture). Lunch. Walks. Peer's Story. Dinner. Lecture. Process. And the list goes on.

Yes, it is therapeutic. I really need this. And by the way, I'll tell my story tomorrow.

I hope all is well with you. I look forward to seeing you the moment I arrive. Give or take a few moments. Foxy first.

Love always,
Michael.[1]

✵   ✵   ✵

I eventually transferred into a "unit" called "Shoemaker." The first person I met there was Larry, also known as Bubba. He was a white football player from Texas who was chemically addicted and was at Hazelden to get clean. He had already been there for twenty-three days and he hated everyone non-white, gay, bi-sexual—you name it, he hated them.

"I hate niggers and faggots!" he told me without blinking.

I thought he was the most adorable thing ever. He had red hair, freckles, and was big and burly. The following fall, he was heading to play fullback for the N.F.L. Of course, this information excited my twisted mind and the next thing you know, he was my roommate.

I endeared myself to him and although we were only roommates for the last five days of his stay at Hazelden, every night we stayed up late playing 500 Gin Rummy, talking about our lives, and having a ton of laughs. I think his twenty-eight days at Hazelden made him a little more introspective because of the types of people he met there. He also signed my Big Book:

Dear Michael,

  I hope when you think of me you smile because you put a smile and peace in my heart that I'll never forget.

                                        I love you,
                                        Bubba.

The day he left, I helped him out to the car with his luggage and we hugged. I sent him off with solid words of peace and twelve-step advice. When I returned to our room, I found he had left his football jersey on my bed. It was one of the most thoughtful gifts I had ever received.

✿   ✿   ✿

Not long after Bubba left, I received a lovely letter from my Aunt Jennie:

My dearest Michael,

I've started this note to you I don't know how many times. I want to be awe-inspiring, I want to take away all your pain. I want to make you well and I want to make you happy. I've never written a letter to a family member except to my husband, Jackie, when he was in the service. However, since receiving your letter, I have felt compelled to respond. First, I have to let you know how very dear you are to me. Since your dad's passing, I hoped that we were bonding. It's very important to me, I'm sure selfishly, that we keep in touch for

whatever time I have left. Now you know I'm not being maudlin. I care for you
unconditionally, What you have done and what you are doing is so together of
you. I'm very proud. I, in short, must tell you that I am here for you any time.

Will write to you again, love,

Titi.[2]

Her letter filled me with such joy, a feeling I had not experienced in
many years because of my addiction. I was starting to learn the importance
of my family's love. I hoped my ability to recognize and accept that would
last after I left Hazelden.

Meanwhile, life there was very strict. There were daily group meetings,
and one-on-one's with your unit counselor. One of the major rules at the
center was that you weren't allowed to speak with anybody who was not in
your unit. The staff insisted on keeping everything organized and under
control, so fraternizing with the other units was strictly verboten.

But being boy crazy, I kept seeing sexy young men in all the other units
and in the locker room—so, of course, I *really* wanted to talk to them.
Luckily, everyone from all the units ate at the same buffet in the dining
room. I particularly remember one guy named Tim. He had a very seventies
rooster-like haircut, similar to Rod Stewart. He had freckles everywhere
with a somewhat athletic build, and I just loved that he worked in construction. After Hazelden, we stayed in touch for many years, mostly on the
telephone—until 2017, when I heard he died from brain cancer.

By January 10, I was counting down the remainder of my days at Hazelden. I had ten more to go. I was anxious to get out. I felt really good
and I knew I would stay sober, that I wouldn't drink or do drugs again if I
followed the program. And that was true—until 1999.

But right then, what mattered more than anything was getting out of
Hazelden and back to New York, because I had to start recording the new
Nina Simone record, her first studio album in years—and what would wind
up being her last.

26

A SINGLE WOMAN

Nina Simone is my favorite artist in all the world. She was a tough cookie to work with and by the time I met her she had already recorded for many record labels and was known for being a difficult diva. It was a gift working with her. She spoke about the beauty and the troubles of life with that world-weary voice that enchanted everyone who heard her sing. The record I executive-produced for her is called *A Single Woman*. It is a record that speaks of love loneliness and loss. It was modeled after Frank Sinatra's record *A Man Alone* [and Billie Holiday's *Lady in Satin*], which we both loved. I thought she was so beautiful and when she smiled all was right with the world . . . but don't get on her bad side cause she had quite a temper and you never knew if she was packing a pistol in her purse. [1]

—Michael Alago

I first heard Nina Simone in my Titi Jennie's living room in Brooklyn when I was about twelve years old. The albums Titi Jennie played were *Live at Town Hall* and *In Concert*—we listened to those recordings over and over again. I was completely overwhelmed by the beauty and intensity of her voice. It had a power and a richness I had never heard before. All of that, even at a very young age, spoke to me. She was on my radar from that moment on.

In June 1983, I was given the incredible gift of actually meeting her. She was performing four shows in two days at Irving Plaza and, for the occasion, the club had renamed itself Swing Plaza. It was a big deal because she hadn't performed in the U.S. in a very long time.

But the obstreperous and brilliant Nina Simone, who returned to New York to sing at Swing Plaza this weekend after a five-year absence, demands more than polite appreciation. Rooted in extreme emotional ambivalence, her performances have the aura of sacramental rites, in which a priestess and her flock work to establish a mystical communion. Because of Miss Simone's fabled temperament, however, communion is not a foregone conclusion. Each performance becomes a group psychodrama that could as easily topple into disaster as soar into triumph. But at Swing Plaza on Friday, Miss Simone triumphed over an obvious case of nerves and physical discomfort to end up smiling.[2]

I had been working at Elektra for about five months and I thought this was a perfect chance to make contact with Nina. I did so by first getting in touch with her brother, Sam Waymon, who was her manager at the time. When I telephoned him, I introduced myself and said I was from Elektra Records and that I adored his sister.

It was arranged that I would go to the sound check at Irving Plaza to meet the famed music and civil rights icon, and I brought along my friend Antone.

When we got there, we stood in the back of the venue. Nina caught sight of us and called us over. I was shaking inside.

"Hi, I'm Michael Alago from Elektra Records." She looked at me skeptically, raising her eyebrows.

"*You?*" she said. "*You're* the A&R man? How *old* are you?"

I laughed nervously and told her that yes, I was the A&R executive, as she eyed me up and down.

"Do you have any money with you?"

"Well, that's not how it works," I said. "I'm just here to introduce myself to you."

"If you don't have any money, then why are you here?"

I started feeling a little uncomfortable. It was definitely awkward, then Antone whispered, "I think we should just go."

"No!" I said. "This is an opportunity of a lifetime."

So we stayed a little while longer and watched the sound check. Antone and I left for dinner, then came back and watched the show, which was awe-inspiring.

Afterwards, I went backstage and she was still a little cold. She didn't say much, then at some point she asked me, "Do you have a ride?"

I quickly turned to Antone.

"Hey, Ms. Simone needs a ride, can you do this?"

"No," he said. "It's almost midnight, I need to get home."

"Antone, this is really, *really* important!"

"But she wants to go to Rockland County! I got to get home!" he said.

Antone finally came to his senses and agreed. We climbed into his car to take Nina to her brother's house in Rockland County.

Nina sat in the front seat while I sat in the back. Antone recalls that she asked if she could smoke and he said yes, but she was still a bit distant and nasty.

Then a few minutes later, she put her cigarette out on the carpet on the floor of the car and flames started shooting up. She had set the car's carpet on fire! Antone *freaked*. He struggled to put out the flames while he drove. It got a little scary but one thing changed and that was Nina. Her attitude completely turned around. She was so upset and embarrassed about burning the carpet that she became very apologetic. She said she felt terrible about it.

✻   ✻   ✻

I really wanted to sign Nina to Elektra. I wanted to bring her back into the spotlight. I had adored her for twenty years and I would do anything to get her on the label. But Kras would have none of it. He thought she was a has-been. He was very stern about it. She hadn't made a record in nearly a decade, and rarely did concerts in the U.S. As far as Bob was concerned, signing her was a ridiculous suggestion.

But I refused to give up, and kept following her. I went to see her at the Olympia in Paris, the Town and Country and Ronnie Scott's Jazz Club in London—*anywhere* I could find her.

I was very compassionate towards Nina. I knew of her drinking and medicating which didn't help her mood swings and which sometimes fueled her anger about the oppression she had seen her people suffer.

She was very pro-black, had come up through the civil rights era of the sixties and had constantly faced humiliating and degrading treatment as a black performer. Once, when she was reminiscing, she told me a story about her first recital at age twelve and how she refused to start singing when her parents were moved from the first row to the back of the auditorium, to make room for whites to sit there.[3]

Black performers were forced to go through the back door of the venues they were playing—there were no overnight accommodations for them, and as we all know, the water fountains were labeled "White Only" and "Colored Only." And this all happened even when they were the headliners of the show that night. That always infuriated Nina.

At the same time, she was not receiving royalties for her albums from a variety of record companies and, adding insult to injury, many of her recordings were bootlegged and sold all over the world. What she saw was people fucking with her music, and she never received one dime from the proceeds.

Her experience as a black performer—as a black woman—caused her to be aggressively outspoken during the civil rights movement, calling for violent revolutions and extreme political activism. She wrote songs condemning the persecution of her people.

Then everything blew up—not only with Medgar Evers' death, but Dr. King's and Malcolm X's. It all fell apart for her. I think she believed she had come through the civil rights movement unsuccessfully and felt very lost after all of those deaths.

She wrote "Mississippi Goddam" in response to the 1963 assassination of Medgar Evers and the Birmingham church bombing that killed four young

African-American girls. She also penned "Four Women," chronicling the complex histories of a quartet of African-American female figures, and "Young, Gifted and Black," borrowing the title of a play by [Lorraine] Hansberry, which became a popular anthem.[4]

In 1986, a few years after her appearance at Irving Plaza, she played nine nights at the Village Gate. I went to almost every show and she was nothing short of brilliant. She looked devastatingly beautiful each night, and every set was totally different. In fact, at one of the shows, I shouted out: "Sing 'Baltimore'!" That was a cut from Randy Newman's 1977 album, *Little Criminals*.

She stopped the performance cold. She looked directly at me and said, in her very affected, highfalutin tone, "We love Randy Newman. But we do not do 'Baltimore.' As a matter of fact, we do not do *anything* from that album. I made that record for $10,000 for Creed Taylor at CTI and he never gave me a dime once that record was released. So, we will not be doing 'Baltimore' this evening."

Everyone laughed nervously, then she fell into "Pirate Jenny," "Porgy," and "Black is the Color of my True Love's Hair."

One evening, toward the end of her run, I went backstage. We were so glad to see each other, we kissed, we hugged, we laughed. Then she looked at me and said, "Oh Michael! You weren't at the show last night!"

"I'm so sorry, my dear, I was at a heavy metal concert."

She covered her mouth and giggled like a small girl. I had brought Kurdt Vanderhoof from Metal Church with me and he obviously looked the part of a heavy metal dude. Nina asked who he was and I told her that he was the guitarist from Metal Church, a group on Elektra. She threw me some shade.

"My dear! Do I have to be in a heavy metal band to get signed to Elektra?"

We all laughed then made a pact to go to the Limelight later that night.

❁   ❁   ❁

We eventually left and went to the Cat Club first. I don't remember when I dropped ecstasy or when I had given Nina some, but I lost her later. When

I went to the Limelight, she was already there. I went over to her and sat down and we ordered a bunch of drinks and giggled and gabbed and gossiped. Around 3 a.m., we decided to leave and Nina asked me to take her to back to her hotel—the Milford Plaza.

However, when we got to the hotel, the night porters and security wouldn't let me go up to Nina's room with her. Nina was wearing a full-length fur coat but I was completely decked out in full leather—a sight that late-night hotel workers kept an extra eye on. However, I was clearly with Nina. Yet they refused to let me go up to the room.

"Where's the manager?" I insisted. "I demand to see the manager!"

"He's not here at this hour, sir."

I was livid. I marched through the door marked "For Employees Only," hunting for the manager. I glared everywhere but found no one.

When I got back to the lobby, Nina suddenly threw her bouquet of roses onto the floor and shouted: "Do you know I am Nina Simone?!" and she spat on the floor. I went over and grabbed her arm.

"Nina, come on! Let's go to the elevator."

We got on the elevator and because we were so high on ecstasy, we were very lovey-dovey with each other:

"Oh, sugar lips!" she cried out to me.

"Honey," I said. "You know how much I love you!"

We then pressed the button for her floor but nothing happened. I pressed it again and again but still nothing. The assholes had turned off the power. We were furious. A few moments later, the police arrived. Clearly the hotel staff had called them to defuse the tense situation.

I was still enraged, but Nina whispered to me, "Maybe you should just go. Call me when you get home." So I stormed out and when I got home around 5 a.m., I called her and we stayed on the phone for the next two hours. It was just one big hoot!

✷   ✷   ✷

In 1992, I was finally able to sign Nina to Elektra.

"You know Bob, I'm never going to let this go," I said to him.

With Bruce Springsteen, 1976.
(Author Collection)

Kissing Deborah Harry backstage
at Max's, 1977.
(Author Collection)

With Arturo Vega in my office at Geffen
Records, 1989. (© Demetrius Constantinus)

At Blondie show, CBGB, 1978.
(Author Collection)

With John Lydon at The Ritz, May, 1981. (Photo courtesy of Pat Kepic)

PiL snapshot, New York City, May, 1981.
(© Michael Alago)

Jerry Brandt, The Ritz, 1981.
(© Michael Alago)

Polaroid of Cliff Burton and Kirk Hammett,
Elektra Records Office, 1984.
(© Michael Alago)

With James Hetfield backstage,
New York, 2018. (Author Collection)

With Lars Ulrich backstage, London, 1984.
(Author Collection)

With Lars Ulrich, New York, 2018.
(Author Collection)

Always fun with Metal Church: Kurdt Vanderhoof, Kirk Arrington, and hiding in the back, vocalist David Wayne (RIP), 1986. (Author Collection)

With Flotsam & Jetsam, New York City, 1986. (Author Collection)

With George Lynch of Dokken, Tokyo, 1988. (Author Collection)

"John and Barking Dog", West Village Piers, New York City, 1981. (© Stanley Stellar)

"Jayson Sucks", West Village Piers, New York City, 1981. (© Stanley Stellar)

Joseph Beuys "Postkarten" box, signed, 1984. (Author Collection)

Polaroid of Beuys' artwork, signed, 1984. (Author Collection)

With Joseph Beuys, Dusseldorf, 1984. (Author Collection)

BJ Robinson, New Orleans, 1979.
(Photo by George Dureau, courtesy of
Arthur Roger Gallery, New Orleans)

Raymond Hall, New Orleans, 1979.
(Photo by George Dureau, courtesy of
Arthur Roger Gallery, New Orleans)

Props used by George Dureau for photo
sessions. I acquired these props at auction.
(Photo courtesy of Crescent City
Auction Gallery, New Orleans)

With George Dureau at The Carrington House,
New Orleans, 2013. (Author Collection)

With Kane Roberts, 2016.
(Author Collection)

Pulling on Doyle's "devil lock,"
Misfits, 2013. (Author Collection)

White Zombie ticket stub from the Marquee
in London, UK, 1992. (Author Collection)

Doyle backstage at the MGM Grand in
Las Vegas, 2017. (© Michael Alago)

With Liza on opening night of "Minnelli on Minnelli," at The Palace Theatre, 1999. (Author Collection)

Swans The Burning World *album cover, 1989. "Calla Lily" photograph by Robert Mapplethorpe. (Author Collection)*

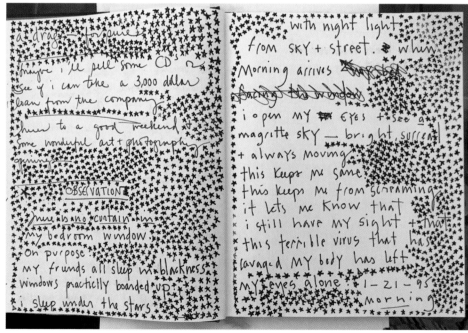

Frenzied journal writing, January, 1995. (Author Collection)

I think he was so damned tired of hearing me talk about her, he threw up his arms up and said, "Just do it already!"

Finally! I had stayed in touch with her throughout the years—I would call her in the South of France or when she visited Accra (in Africa). Then she would call me back at Elektra, demanding to speak to me immediately.

I had massive success at the label with Metallica and, with that success, Bob trusted me to either sink or swim with all my future signings, and I fully intended to swim. After he gave me the green light to sign Nina, I called her representative, Steven Ames Brown. He was a tough negotiator but always veered on the side of decency. He also looked after many black artists of the fifties and sixties who were forced to go through the backdoor years previously. He had to be uncompromising about getting them their money. That was the focus of these extraordinary and creative artists—it always boiled down to money.

I ended up talking with Steven and connected him with Gary Casson, Elektra's head of business affairs—and they closed the deal for Nina.

✻   ✻   ✻

When I started to work on Nina's record, the first thing we needed to do was to find a producer. I set up meetings in the conference room at the Elektra office in Los Angeles, where we interviewed a few potential candidates.

We first met with Tommy Lipuma. A very prominent producer who had worked with Barbra Streisand, Miles Davis, Natalie Cole, and George Benson, among others. I thought he was a perfect choice for Nina's album.

The meeting didn't go well and after he left, Nina turned to me rather deliberately and said, "I don't want no gimp workin' on my record!"

I looked at her, trying to hide my shock.

"What did you say?!"

"I have a brother who's a gimp. I cannot deal with people who have disabilities."

"Okay," I said walking to the other side of the room. "I don't want to talk about this anymore because you're rude, and it doesn't make me feel good about you at all."

The next producer we met with was Andre Fischer. He was the drummer for Rufus featuring Chaka Khan, and at that time was married to Natalie Cole. When he opened the door, Nina was immediately impressed.

A handsome, light-skinned black man—the moment he walked in, he got down on one knee, took Nina's hand and kissed it. He was a big fan of hers and I knew that, in her mind, he could do no wrong. I also knew there was no way she would meet with anyone else. We had lunch together and, afterwards, shook hands. It was a done deal. Andre was the producer.

Nina hadn't made a studio album in nearly eight years. I knew she wanted to make a record about love, loneliness, and loss. I was still carrying the loss of my dad from the previous year, and I felt like we were connected on an emotional level with that record.

At this point we started talking about various types of music. She loved the 1958 album *Lady in Satin* by Billie Holiday, which Billie recorded for Columbia with the Ray Ellis Orchestra. I was incredibly fond of that record, as well.

At the time of that recording, Billie's voice was shot—she was in her mid-40's and in bad health. In fact, she died a year later. *Lady in Satin* wound up being the last album released in her lifetime.

Another album we both loved was Frank Sinatra's *A Man Alone: The Words & Music of McKuen*, recorded in 1969. The songs we were specifically interested in were "Love's Been Good to Me," "Lonesome Cities," and the title track "A Man Alone." We loved that track so much we thought it would be perfect to turn it into a song from a woman's point of view. I suggested to Nina that we change the title of the song, "A Man Alone" to "A Single Woman" and make it the title of her album.

I called Rod McKuen about using a couple of songs from that album and he was over the moon when he heard Nina Simone would be recording his work. He absolutely adored her. He said he had seen her perform when he was a young man in Provincetown at the A-House, and from that day on, she completely blew his mind. He was more than happy to approve the use of all the songs we had requested, including the change in the perspective of "A Man Alone" and how that affected the lyrics, and for that, we were truly grateful.

Nina did not like the idea of titling the album "A Single Woman" at all. "People are going to look at me and think that I'm just old and *single!*"

I argued with her: "No, it gives you a sense of power. You're saying, 'I am a single woman, I'm strong and I'm proud!'"

She eventually gave into the idea and it was decided we would model the recording on both Sinatra and Holiday's records.

We were now finally in the studio with producer Andre Fischer and a very large orchestra. We struggled a lot with Nina's vocals because her voice was not what it used to be. She just couldn't hit certain notes anymore. She was initially embarrassed that her voice was not up to par. Time and age, coupled with the fact that she hadn't been in the studio and around a producer in years, all made working with her difficult.

There was a lot of splicing of tape to get the vocals to be spot-on. It was a huge effort and an immense amount of time on Andre's part to get her voice to the point where it sounded like it did at its peak. When he played it back to her, Nina would say: "*See!* I *told* you I was sounding good!" I looked over to Andre and winked.

By that time, Andre was stretched to the limit. Getting the vocals correct proved to be very demanding, so no matter how poor we felt she sounded, and how much work we were doing—to keep her cool and calm in the studio, we just kept telling her: "Yes, Nina—you sound *great!*"

We finally finished the record toward the middle of 1993, and Nina loved it.

Yes, A Single Woman is about love, all kinds of love. Especially, a full grown woman in love. A woman in the process of defining her life, deciding her fate, accepting, without shame or guilt, her own needs and desires . . . Depending on how well we have been loved or not loved, these lyrics and the earned authority of Simone's voice will bring hope, reassurance, or the right to grieve.[5]

However, the overall reaction to A Single Woman was mixed.

Incomparable and unfathomable, Nina Simone is in her finest form when tearing into the guts and pathos of unlikely songs—by the likes of Bob Dylan, Kurt Weill and Screamin' Jay Hawkins . . . But overall, A Single Woman aims to do nothing more than entertain pleasantly, and that's the one thing Nina Simone, effortless when provoking, grousing or despairing, just can't do.[6]

Nina promised to do a lot of press to promote the album, except she ended up only doing two interviews. One was a huge piece in the *New York Times* by James Gavin.

Nina Simone has just released her first major album in fifteen years, and she is doing everything possible to stand in the way of its success. . . . But none of this is unusual for Ms. Simone, a cult diva whose shamanistic hold on audiences is matched by an infamous temperament. . . . Lavishly arranged for strings, [*A Single Woman*] avoids the political rallying that has dominated much of her work to concentrate on themes of solitude and yearning. Dark, brooding versions of standards like "If I Should Lose You" and "The Folks Who Live on the Hill" are combined with several newer songs, one of which is a searing rendition of "Papa, Can You Hear Me?" from the movie "Yentl." That song holds special meaning for Ms. Simone, whose father died in 1971. "Nina and I had both lost our fathers," says Michael Alago, the album's executive producer. "Issues of love, loneliness and loss kept coming up. I knew that was the kind of record we were going to make.[7]

Nina was hugely volatile, which she was well known for and, although our friendship became unbelievably close, I was not immune to her rude, hurtful outbursts.

A few months after the album was released, I read about an incident in the *New York Post*: "Diva's Home on Fire."

Apparently, there had been a fire that had taken over Nina's house. I immediately called her. However, for some reason, she wouldn't take my call. I asked her housekeeper, Juanita, about it: "How come she doesn't want to talk to me? What's this fire I read about in the *New York Post*?"

"Oh, she won't talk to you—she said you started the fire!"

"How could I start a fucking fire? I'm at 75 Rockefeller Plaza! And you're in the South of France! Can somebody tell me what the *real* story is?"

"Well," said Juanita, "part of the story is you faxed her all day long and she said, tell Michael Alago, I'm not a white man! I'm not a business man. I'm an artist! And what does he want?"

"You tell Nina, I was faxing her all day because I want to send her the rest of her advance!"

Suddenly, Nina piped in.

"Oh, honey! Is that *you* on the phone!?" she cried.

"Nina, have you been on the phone this whole time?

"Oh, no! I picked it up just now!"

"Well, whatever—I didn't start that fire," I said.

Apparently, she had been drinking and her cigarette fell down on the staircase when she was going upstairs to go to sleep, and it set the linen closet on fire.

"Well, there *was* a fire here!" she screamed. "And you know, there was a man who tried to get in my window! He was trying to fuck me!"

"Nina!" I said. "That man wasn't trying to fuck you! He was a fireman, he was trying to save your life!"

"Child!" she cried back. "You're gay! You don't know—*everyone* wants to fuck a black woman!"

"Whatever, Nina—he was there to *save your life!*"

A couple years later, I caught another story in the *New York Post* about Nina. There was a teenager wandering in her backyard and Nina shot at him with a BB gun. I immediately called her about it:

"Nina, I heard you shot someone!"

She came back in a deadpan sigh. "Only in the leg. That kid was lucky! Because, you know, I turned killer a long time ago! And I have a gun under my pillow!" That was the level of drama with her—all the time.

❉   ❉   ❉

Around November of 1993—a few months after *A Single Woman* was released, I went out to L.A. for Nina's appearance on *The Tonight Show* with Jay Leno.

Unfortunately, nothing was ever easy with her. Everything was wrought with extreme tension. We arrived at the studio and went into the Green Room and, right away, she demanded to know if she was getting paid.

"Of course you're getting paid," I told her. "But you're going to have to sign an agreement. We're dealing with a union and they need written approval of your appearance. Then they will mail a check to you. I think the fee is $750."

She looked at me.

"How do I know I'm going to get that money?" she insisted.

"Are you *kidding* me?" I said. "This is NBC. You're going to get your money."

She went on and on about this and it turned out, the door to the room was ajar. Apparently, Jay Leno had been walking by at that moment, and heard everything. He stuck his head into the room and said hello, very graciously. I smiled back.

"Are you Michael Alago from Elektra Records?" he asked me.

"Yes," I replied, trying not to sound nervous.

"May I please speak to you for a moment?"

"Sure," I said, and I followed him out to another Green Room across the hall, thinking to myself the whole time, "Oh my God, did he actually hear what was going on between me and Nina?"

Mr. Leno shut the door after we entered the room.

"What was all that about, I just heard?"

And in the most professional way I could, I explained that Nina had gone through a lot of financial abuse over the years and was super distrustful about getting paid for any performances, appearances, or anything. Money was a big issue for her. He nodded, hearing me, but he was basically not interested.

"Okay," he said. "Is she going to sign the union agreement?"

"I hope so."

"I hope so too." Leno replied.

At that point he seemed totally aggravated. Even though I had tried to keep things as cool as possible, it definitely got a little heated between us.

He then left, and I went back to Nina.

"You really have to sign the union agreement Nina," I said to her, hoping she would agree.

"I *refuse!*" she screamed back at me. "I ain't signin' anything! I want my money!"

A few minutes later, a very angry Jay Leno returned. He slammed open the door.

"May I speak with you again, Mr. Alago?"

We went back to the room across the hall, and he pulled $750 in cash out of his wallet and placed it in my hand. Then he turned and walked out. I was a nervous wreck. He didn't have to do that. He could've just pulled the plug and not have her on the show at all.

I went back to Nina and threw the money on the table. I was furious.

"Here's the $750! Sign the agreement! I don't want to talk about it. You're going to go on! Leno's going to do a short interview with you after you sing the title track to the record."

The taping for the show started. When the other guest segments were finished, Leno introduced Nina. She went on to perform "A Single Woman" and when she finished, she stood up from the piano and took a bow. Leno went over to her, took her hand, and walked her back to the dais. Unfortunately, Nina performed at the end of the show, so there was no time for an on-air interview. But she did get to sing and Leno was very gracious to her. I was so relieved it was finished.

The record didn't do very well and it didn't help that Nina refused to promote it. Elektra Records had bigger fish to fry. Bob let me know I had to tell Nina the label was releasing her from her contract.

She was furious. I apologized a million times.

"You got a huge advance!" I reminded her. "And we made a great record!" She was in no way pacified.

"Don't they know who I *am!*?" she screamed.

I sighed, and said to her, "Every time I suggested something to you that we needed to do to promote the album, you flat out said 'no.'"

She was livid, but there was nothing I could do.

It broke my heart. As an artist, I adored her. It was never easy working with her, but her music was everything to me.

✿   ✿   ✿

Sunday
July 11, 1993
At Home
At Bouc-Bel-Air

Dear Michael,

I have an hour to talk to you. That's all. I have thought about this all night and it's time. You <u>insulted</u> me with your letter. I don't want to lose you, that's why I'm taking the time. I told Jim to tell you weeks ago that I wanted no more <u>Americans</u> over here—cause they're all full of tricks. And at that time you were no exception but I paid (for the very last time) 10,000 hard earned dollars to get a bodyguard over here.

I was attracted to you because you were innocent to a real woman and I <u>knew</u> that you were gay (yes). But you were sweet. I knew it might not go anywhere, but in <u>America,</u> it was better than having nothing.

Okay—let's move on. Don't ever tell me again about my age which you nor anyone else should ever <u>have known</u>. Don't give me advice about my medica-tion + alcohol. I've <u>done all that Michael Alago</u>. You obviously are having re-lapses about when <u>you</u> were on drugs. I've even taken drugs, and the Trilafon you + everybody else talks about (only in <u>America,</u> I might add) had made me a zombie for 5 years, thanks to little Mark and my dead father, I found a Dr. who took me off the stuff. Now what you've done is listen to all this bullshit (forgetting that I'm a passionate woman) Michael—Do you hear? I don't show my <u>legs</u> for nothing. These songs are for men—men. Even little Mark <u>wanted me</u> + told me so. He used to massage me, feed me, clothe me, shop for me + clean + cook for me. Okay?

I knew the French loved me. I've known it for 20 years. When the fire was here, it was they who helped me + just this morning, a man + his son got on the roof + replaced one of the roof (rocks) that had leaked water from when the bodyguard was up there.

<u>Lastly</u>, I played + sang the record. What the hell is Elektra (with their mil-lions) doing to promote it? Where will the posters be—in what stores. Where in the world—what magazines are they advertising in? You had enthusiasm, I had talent—it's their fucking job to promote it. "Point of No Return" is being

promoted all over Aix-en-Provence it starts July 14th. I'm not impressed by Elektra. I've been with many record companies. If they wanted they could get a hold of all my past records + use them (plus the photographs which you <u>say</u> you'll get) to launch a major campaign. Why is all this shit up to me? That's not fair + I'm not <u>buying</u> it. I won't be calling you, Michael. I have no fax, no telephone + today no electricity. <u>Mark Penniman</u> bless his heart, came over here and got to the roots of things. I said I had no time for business. But I get <u>upset</u> when you Americans write me things. And I'm interested in my <u>money</u>.

Learn to <u>respect</u> me, Michael, like Jim and Mark do + maybe we can still be friends + make Elektra do its job!

I'm a Doctor of Humanities from Malcolm X College and a Doctor of Music from Amherst College! Did you know that? <u>Mark</u> is the only one who's come over here + helped me and saw my <u>needs</u>. He wanted to take care of <u>all of them</u>. But I'll wait for Africa! where I hope to go July 24th. I need a lover all the time + with "Dr. Feelgood" (As Aretha says "there is no more need for pills of any kind")

Write me—

*Love
Nina.*[8]

Two Years Later—*Phone Call with Nina, February, 1995:*

Me: Happy New Year! How are you?

Nina: I'm doing fine.

Me: I've been thinking of you, you must forgive me—is today your birthday, or the twenty-third?

Nina: Yesterday.

Me: Yesterday! Oh! I missed it by one day! Happy Birthday!

Nina: Thank you, darling . . .

Me: How have you been in general?

Nina: Well, I've been sick.

Me: Like, with the flu?

Nina: Well, no, I had something much more serious than that. I had surgery.

Me: Oh, Nina, I'm sorry . . . are you recovering okay from it?

Nina: I'm recovering.

Me: Thank God. I'm glad to hear that.

Nina: The doctor said I can't work till September . . .

Me: Did you know that I finally met Lisa here recently?

Nina: How did you do that?

Me: I was on a business trip in Chicago and she was in the production of *Rent* and I went to see it and I saw that she was listed there . . .

Nina: She was great in it.

Me: Did you ever get that big jar of peppers that I sent you? Ha-ha! I thought it's so big, I gotta send that to Nina, she'll get a kick out of it.

Nina: Yeah, I use it, too.

Me: Good! I'm glad to hear that. . . . well, you've just been on my mind so much . . . because it's February and it's your birthday and I'm glad you're recovering, so you'll stay now in the South of France till your full recovery?

Nina: Yes, I will, and meanwhile I'll go to Africa sometime between now and September. I bought some land down there. I have a number-one hit in Holland right now.

Me: With what?

Nina: "Ain't Got No, I Got Life."

Me: Really? Was it reissued on a record or something?

Nina: Uh, an insurance company put it out.

Me: Oh, on a commercial?

Nina: On a commercial.

Me: Wow! So you made money from it?

Nina: Yeah.

Me: Damn right. Good, good. I'm happy to hear that.

Nina: It was 11 and now it's going to number 1.

Me: Wow! What label would put it out in Holland, do you know?

Nina: BMG

Me: BMG—yes, that's right!

Nina: Well, thank you for calling, my sugar.

Me: You're always in my thoughts, my prayers . . . I think the absolute world of you, Nina, and I always want the best for you and, uh, like I said, I'm just calling to give you a big kiss, to say Happy Birthday and try to be in touch when you can.[9]

✻   ✻   ✻

The last time I saw Nina was in July of 1999. She was doing a concert in London. She was part of the Meltdown Festival music series at The Royal Festival Hall, being promoted by Nick Cave from the band The Bad Seeds. Artists from all genres—featuring Alan Vega, Elvis Costello, Lee Hazelwood, and, of course, Nina Simone—were appearing:

> Now 66, Simone is a bulky, forbidding figure who seizes complete control of the stage despite the fact that she can walk only with difficulty. As she launched into "Black is the Colour," you didn't need to be a professor of musicology to work out that her voice is barely a husk of its former self, shorn of such luxuries as pitch and intonation . . . [w]hat her performance has, though, is an uncompromising rawness, and an implicit attitude that says, "If you don't like it, °°°° you."[10]

On the afternoon of her show, I showed up at The Ritz in Piccadilly where she was staying. I arrived with two dozen white roses and a bottle of champagne because I knew she would love both of them. I hadn't seen her in a while and we were both thrilled to see each other.

There was a lot of activity in her room. A few people were making sure her clothes were pressed; another woman was cornrowing her hair, braiding it close to her scalp so she could wear a turban for that evening's performance. But once she saw me, she kicked everyone out of the room and threw open her arms. We hugged, we kissed, and then she said to me, "Oh, my dear, we should take a bubble bath!"

"*What?*" I asked, a little shocked. But then I thought to myself, *Well, it is Nina Simone—we're going to take a bubble bath.*

I went into the bathroom and checked the medicine cabinet, but of course—no bubbles. I called the concierge and asked them to call the chemist and see if they have any bubble bath products and, if so, would they purchase it, put it on the bill, and bring it up to Nina Simone's room.

After the porter brought the bottle to us, I poured it into the tub and waited for the bubbles to rise up. Nina came in, and without a thought took off all her clothes and climbed into the bathtub. I wasn't too hot about taking off all my clothes, so I kept my boxers on and got in with her.

I had brought the champagne with me and poured out two glasses. We started drinking and laughing and telling each other completely silly stories. We felt totally free, without a care in the world.

Eventually, the bubbles disappeared, and we climbed out of the tub. Her assistants and hair stylist returned to dress her and finish her hair.

I gave her a big kiss and left. I returned to the hotel at 6 p.m. to take her to the show at The Royal Festival Hall. She rose to the occasion that night. Her performance was unspeakably remarkable.

[T]he most spine-tingling number of all is 'Four Women', a defiant song about the legacy of slavery. Here we have vintage Simone, staring into the abyss. This is where her genius lies—in her ability to take the listener right through pain, and then transcend it. The stark, lyrical images and the brooding intensity of her voice makes a feted pop/soul newcomer such as Lauryn Hill seem like a mere pretender. There is such supreme conviction, such a definitive quality in the way Simone sings "My skin is black/My hair is woolly", as if hers is the last word.[11]

After I saw her in London that year, we stayed in touch through phone calls and letters.

During this Third Act in Nina's life, she continued to perform and make appearances. She also sued and tackled every record company and publisher that hadn't paid her fairly over the years. By early 2003, she owned two homes, was receiving royalties on a multimillion-dollar catalogue, and was playing to audiences of thousands all around the world. She had become comfortable in her own skin and grateful for the recognition she was receiving as the true icon she was.

In April of 2003, as I was walking to the subway on 8th Avenue to go to my dad's grave, which I do every year in the spring to clean it and plant new flowers—something stopped me and told me to call Nina. The feeling I had was very strong.

I went back to my apartment, put my stuff down, took off my coat, and called the South of France.

Juanita answered the phone and I asked to speak to Nina.

"You know, Michael, it's Dr. Simone." (She insisted on being referred to as Dr. ever since she was awarded the honorary doctorates.)

So, I followed protocol and said, "Can Dr. Simone come to the phone, please?"

"Well, you know, Michael, about all the procedures and everything," Juanita continued.

Nina had been battling breast cancer for a long time and she recently had a small stroke.

"I just want to say hello."

Juanita put the phone up to Nina's ear and I said, "Hey, Nina! It's Michael! I love you!"

"Oh, sugar lips! How are ya'?" Nina whispered.

"I'm good, but you don't sound so great, honey."

"I'm not doing too good," she said. "I don't know why you never ever married me!"

"Well, you know I totally adore you and I'm going to come and visit you tomorrow."

There was a sudden silence on the other end of the phone which made me think we may have talked a little too long. Juanita came back on and said:

"You know, Michael, she's very weak."

"I understand," I replied. "Is her assistant, Clifton, there?"

"No," she said.

"Will you please let Clifton know that I'm getting on a plane tomorrow to Marseille? And that someone needs to pick me up at the airport to take me to Carry-le-Rouet, Bouches-du-Rhône? And here's my number if he has to call me and, just so you know, I'm getting on the first plane out in the morning."

We hung up. I went to the cemetery, returned home, and started packing. Later, when I went to sleep, I forgot that I had left the computer on and when I woke up, I noticed the CNN homepage on the screen. The headline read: "Nina Simone, Dead at 70."

I was wrecked, a complete mess. I tried to call her house, but I couldn't get through. I emailed, but got no response. No one contacted me about the funeral either—not Clifton; not Roger, the head of her fan club; not her daughter, Lisa—*no one*. They all knew of my relationship with Nina, but no one contacted me. I was surprised and deeply hurt.

Finally, I had to let it go. I knew, personally, what I had with Nina was very special. It still amazes me how I had become so infatuated with her at the age of twelve, and then, as an adult, was given the chance to work with this truly incomparable artist. That was my life with Nina Simone, and I adored her.

Every generation has to discover Nina Simone. She is evidence that female genius is real," [said] Germaine Greer . . . [s]he sings about women's love—that great, unmanageable, obscene thing.[12]

27

I DREAMED I DRANK A NIGHTMARE

Don't you get it? You frightened young man. AIDS didn't start with Rock
Hudson. It was around long before either of us heard about it.[1]

In 1992, I met Brian Regnaert at Bill's Bar in Boston. He was working
as a bartender while trying to get his modeling career going. I met him
through my friend, Jeff Marshall, who was also tending bar with Brian.
Later, Jeff told me about his friend Demetrius who owned a small shop
on Newbury street called The Gods. A fellow photographer, Demetrius
had taken a number of photos of Brian that he wanted to show me. When
I saw them, I thought, "What a stunning creature!" Such a great beauty.
Brian had been photographed for Guess Jeans by Bruce Weber and was
becoming more sought after by many photographers. We became fast
friends. It was a chemical thing, an inexplainable draw—we really enjoyed
being together. Although we became very close, it never turned romantic—even if I hoped it would.

Eventually, Brian said he wanted to move to New York. His career was
picking up and he wanted to make a mark in the big city.

"Why don't you come stay with me?" I said to him.

"*Really*?" he asked.

"*Sure*! You can stay as long as you need—until you find your own place."

He was very excited. There was an innocence about him wanting to move to the city, and I expect he was thinking: "Oh, I get to go to New York! I can live with Michael Alago 'cause he invited me!"

When Brian finally arrived in 1993, he quickly moved in. We had home-cooked dinners almost every night—mostly pasta, because it was easy. I usually created a very tasty tomato basil sauce which I made from scratch. We ate these dinners while watching movies on TV. It began to feel like a safe and warm home life.

We were also at concerts and the theatre all the time. I took him backstage to everything. We went to see the Rolling Stones, Patti Smith, and Sisters of Mercy; we even went to Joey Ramone's birthday party, where we hung out with him at his apartment. We loved going out to all the downtown cultural events as well as to movies. At one point we saw the film, *True Romance*, which became Brian's favorite. Over the course of these few months, it turned into one of the most significant friendships of my life, and even more importantly, because he was there when I started to get sick.

By 1994, AIDS was the leading cause of death in the United States for people between the ages of 25 and 44.[2] "Sex was dangerous. Blood was a killer. No one was truly safe. . . . 41,669 United States citizens were dead due to complications from AIDS."[3]

Although I had been asymptomatic since 1983 when I was diagnosed as HIV-positive, in 1992, I had a bout of the mumps. I thought it was a little strange that someone in their early thirties would develop a childhood disease, and it seemed strange to my doctor, Barbara Starrett, as well. I recovered from it and felt fine, but that was the beginning of my AIDS nightmare.

About four months after Brian moved in, the illness reared its ugly head again. I developed anemia; I started shitting constantly and was unable to keep anything down. So, of course, I started to lose weight; in fact, I was wasting away. I had an 18 T-cell count, which basically meant I didn't have an immune system at all. I also noticed my chest becoming heavy. I felt shaky, and my thoughts became a bit manic. Anything and everything was attacking my body.

I remember when I first told Brian I was sick. We were sitting out on my terrace enjoying a warm summer sun as it disappeared behind the buildings. It was a hard thing to tell him, and I could feel my tears welling up.

"I don't know how to tell you this—" I said.

"What?"

"I'm positive."

"Positive?"

"HIV positive," I said to him. "I have HIV."

There was a long pause and then as my tears started spilling out, Brian began crying too. He said he had never known anyone with HIV—he knew about the disease—but it had never hit so close to home. He was devastated.

Being HIV-positive is a confirmation that HIV antibodies have been activated; it does not mean that person has—or will have—AIDS. Detectable antibodies in the bloodstream are spirits of the brave cells lost as they waged a battle against the virus. Before labs could measure the amount of virus in a person's blood, the Center for Disease Control ("CDC") created a somewhat arbitrary baseline of 200 CD4+ T-lymphocytes ("T-cells") to distinguish immuno-decline.[4]

This was at a time when all my male friends, in and out of the music business, were dying. I was filled with fear. There was no cure. There was no solution.

Because of my 18 T-cell count, one of the first things to hit me was PCP pneumonia.[5] Dr. Starrett started me on Pentamidine[6] inhalers, which I took to work with me and used behind closed doors. But very quickly, it was clear that the medication wasn't working. I was getting worse. She immediately started me on intravenous Pentamidine.

Dr. Starrett insisted I go to the hospital immediately. But I absolutely refused. I fought tooth and nail not to go into the AIDS ward at St. Vincent's Hospital. The situation in the ward was dire. I had so much fear that, to me, going into the AIDS ward signaled death.

Smoking, sun damage, tooth decay, politics, blocked calls, money troubles, talk of a cure: these are just some of the things you no longer care about when your doctor has given up on you and you're one of a chorus of guys awaiting your big death number on the 7th floor of St. Vincent's.[7]

Luckily, I had the best health insurance. I had fifteen to eighteen days of a private nurse coming to my home and, even more fortunately, Brian was there.

Brian's mother was a nurse. When he was growing up, he went with her to visit patients in the hospital. He was raised with a real sense of caring for others and, in many unforeseen ways, he was heaven-sent.

So, I stayed home. Barbara accepted it, even though she didn't like the idea of it at all. Then she started doing the most beautiful thing. Every morning at 5 a.m., before she made her rounds at St. Vincent's, she rode her bike to my apartment to check up on me. It was incredible. She organized it so the visiting nurse would give me the I.V. Pentamidine for the PCP pneumonia, and Brian would give me three intramuscular injections of Procrit per week for the anemia. I was still on an I.V. drip of vitamins and pills that would "help" the immune system. I don't remember what the pills were and I don't know if I really cared at the time. I had that panic that we all had in the gay community then—to get any medication we heard about which might save our lives.[8] It was very *Dallas Buyers Club* everywhere.

At one point, I developed toxoplasmosis in the brain, which is a parasite.[9] I had to take pyrimethamine and sulfonamides to get rid of it. The infection and medication kept me awake constantly. I couldn't sleep for two or three days at a time. My whole system felt dreadful. I was a nervous wreck. I had so much anxiety. I had no idea what to do with it. I wrote frantically in my journal:

I hate this nervous energy from no sleep.
  My handwriting is changing since the pneumonia.
  Since the pneumonia I haven't found a comfortable rhythm to settle into yet—need to find it soon so I don't go crazy.

These hours I'm keeping are crazy, 5:30 in the morning is too damn early to do anything! Never mind, I'm up and ready to go like it was the fucking army! Yuck!

What to do?

Read.

Write.

God helps us all.

Please.

Silence is not needed.

Wow, that Klonopin tablet sent me into outer space for the evening. That's good, I guess.

It's 5 a.m. I took another Klonopin to see how it feels. Dr. Starrett wants me to take 3 a day, which sounds extreme. We'll see how I feel.

Should I try to sleep more? I'll give it a try. I want to write a book. The book will be called "Love and Death From the Virus." Sounds good to me.

I got a good boxing photo from Ira.

I need a new typewriter.

I have a new poem here—"In the Garden."

It's 3:20 a.m. and it's a ridiculous hour to be up, but here I am again. And the smell of bananas repulses me. I'll never eat a fucking banana again.

I took another Klonopin and I hope to be in dreamland shortly.

Where are people going at 3:30 in the morning?

I'm still not sleeping. I see headlights outside. Street lights. What's going to become of this sleep pattern?

I need to set up my work table for collage and typing but it's already put together in my bedroom.

Writing with a better typewriter would help. Get a better typewriter ASAP.

I'm not sleeping from that second Klonopin.

Writing, I never thought so much of it in my life. It will be my salvation.

Saw Matthew Goulet—psychiatrist—thorough, smart, and very handsome. Both doctors want to desensitize me to Bactrim again, also to get a CAT Scan and a spinal tap.

This is hell.

It's 4:30 in the morning again. I did get 8 hours of sleep. but still. . .

I'm takin Klonopin, I'm writing postcards, I made a tape for Patti

5:30 in the morning!

Where are all of these trucks going? What are they delivering? Deliver me
a boy is more like it!
I feel like shit. I hope its temporary.
I'll go to sleep early and start eating more greens
I Think I Want to Live in a Treehouse.[10]

✵   ✵   ✵

The anemia and the toxoplasmosis and the anxiety kept me chained to the
sofa. I couldn't get up to do anything. If I had to get up I could only do it
slowly, like I was a very, very old man. I hobbled to the bathroom, and then
back to the sofa, and then back to the bathroom, the sofa, the bathroom,
the sofa. . . .

> There is no curtain in my bedroom window . . . on purpose
> My friends all sleep in blackness
> Windows practically boarded up
> I sleep under the stars with nightlight
> From sky and street
> When morning arrives
> I open my eyes
> To see a Magritte sky
> Bright, surreal and always moving
> This keeps me sane
> This keeps me from screaming
> It lets me know
> That I still have my sight
> And that this terrible virus
> That has ravaged my body
> Has left my eyes alone.
> I am the keen observer of truth and beauty.[11]

Because I couldn't get up easily and Brian was often out running errands
or going on auditions—when the phone rang, he wasn't around to pick it up
for me. I couldn't get up to answer it myself, so my answering machine re-

corded whatever calls came in. Some of them were very long and involved. Many were from friends and family, as well as Chris Duffy—my boyfriend at the time, Nina Simone, or Patti Smith.

The medication and the toxoplasmosis were still keeping me crazed. I even called Michael Feinstein in the middle of the night because he was heading to the White House in the morning to perform. I asked him to steal President Clinton's cat "Socks" when he got there. In fact, I begged him.

"You have to get me that cat! Bring me back Socks!"

He heard me loud and clear, but then tried to talk me down from my late-night mania. And when he came back, all he brought me was a fuckin' napkin with the White House logo on it. No Socks! No silverware! Nothing! I was furious.

Around this time, Barbara told me about a new medication that the FDA had approved called AZT.[12] She said I could take a small amount to see if I could tolerate it, and then take a larger amount later that would, theoretically, help the AIDS symptoms, which were by then exploding.

> Burroughs Wellcome . . . tested . . . something called Compound S, a re-made version of the original AZT. When it was thrown into a dish with animal cells infected with HIV, it seemed to block the virus' activity.[13]

The problem was that many of the men I knew who were taking AZT were dying or had died from the very drug that was supposed to save them.

> Under enormous public pressure, the FDA's review of AZT was fast tracked . . . [a]fter 16 weeks, Burroughs Wellcome announced that they were stopping the trial because there was strong evidence that the compound appeared to be working.[14]

Barbara was skeptical about it. But she was willing to give me the AZT if I wanted it.

> You will not find a more potent symbol of the complex story of AZT, a story of how the struggle to find a "magic bullet" to help millions of people . . . degenerated into a saga of distrust, confusion, and anger. It is a story of health

and illness . . . of scientific ambition, secrecy and political pressure, and of the amounts of money that can be generated when a lethal virus turns into a worldwide epidemic.[15]

Barbara knew there was something wrong with the drug as she was seeing too many deaths related to it. I think, somewhere in her mind, she believed there would be a new medication soon. I knew how smart she was so I continued doing all the nontraditional things she recommended.

I don't remember how many months passed that I was incredibly ill, lying on the sofa. There were many times in the middle of the night when Brian had to arrange for a taxi to take me to the hospital. He usually called the gang in my inner circle to help: Debbie Southwood Smith, Carol Friedman, Arturo Vega, Tim Ebneth and Daniel Rey—these marvelous people were, like Brian, selflessly concerned for me. There were nights when Debbie came over to my apartment because I had a fever so high I could barely function. She would wash me down with cool, wet towels and change my sheets and stay with me until the fever broke. Often Arturo and Daniel came by during the day to lift my spirits and sit quietly with me and watch TV. I was constantly on the phone with Carol, and sometimes both Eric Bogosian and Tim Ebneth came over to keep me company and bring me muffins and sweets. I was wasting away and all my friends just wanted to see me healthy again.

Then in the middle of the year, on one of her morning visits, Barbara told me about a number of drugs she had learned about which she believed held real promise. Among them was a Protease inhibitor called Saquinavir, and she urged me to take it. I don't think it had been approved by the FDA yet,[16] but she believed it was the right thing for me to take. She also urged me to take it in combination with a few other drugs, an early form of the "cocktail," I believe, which ultimately became the primary treatment for HIV patients.

In 1995, a combination drug treatment known as the "AIDS cocktail" was introduced. This type of therapy is now known as highly active antiretroviral therapy (HAART). . . . [which] has led to dramatic improvements in people who have used it. People have experienced decreased viral loads (the amount of HIV in their body) and increased counts of CD4 cells (immune cells that are destroyed by HIV). According to the Centers for Disease Control and Prevention, people who take antiretroviral therapy as prescribed and maintain an undetectable viral load have "effectively no risk" of transmitting HIV to others.[17]

I had enormous faith in her. She had accepted that I would not go to the AIDS ward in St. Vincent's; she supported me by coming every day to check on me at my home; and she had steered me away from AZT. There was no way I wouldn't follow her recommendation, so I took the medications.

With introduction of highly active antiretroviral therapy, AIDS diagnoses and deaths declined substantially from 1995 to 1998 and remained stable from 1999 to 2008 at an average of 38,279 AIDS diagnoses and 17,489 deaths per year, respectively.[18]

About six months later, I started to feel better. Brian had moved out by that time and taken an apartment on East 27th Street. Around that time, I went over to his place for his thirtieth birthday to celebrate with his family. I did not look my best. I was still thin and gaunt, but I felt strong. My gratitude to Brian is immeasurable. It was hard to understand the kind of selfless gift he gave in being there when I was so close to dying. He was a saint in helping me to recover and to survive, because as I sat there while he blew the candles out on his birthday cake, I felt it coming back. It was all coming back—my strength, my health . . . my life.

❊   ❊   ❊

Those years, in the early 1980s when AIDS first hit, were a frightening time for all of us. The fear was monstrous in size and it took over the entire community. We were struggling with symptoms that were unimaginably painful and devastating. There was also the uncertainty and threat of medications doctors were trying and hoping to get approved faster than light, to stop this catastrophic plague.

However, there was a feeling—at least in the beginning—that we, the gay community, somehow brought this horrific disease into the world. That belief remained, despite the fact that AIDS was destroying many, and for a time, nearly all of us in that world. Thankfully, that judgment was disproven.

> SIVcpz [simian virus] was transferred to humans as a result of chimps being killed and eaten, or their blood getting into cuts or wounds on people in the course of hunting. Normally, the hunter's body would have fought off SIV, but on a few occasions the virus adapted itself within its new human host and became HIV-1 . . . which is the strain that has spread throughout the world and is responsible for the vast majority of HIV infections today.[19]

Today, I take a cocktail of medications like every other person with HIV, and I stay healthy. I have safe sex, and I deal in strength and faith, and antivirals, because there is always a tomorrow for me and there is always hope in that tomorrow.

> Vito [Russo] gave a speech to ACT-UP in 1988 that would become his boilerplate pep talk. "Someday, the AIDS Crisis will be over," he would shout to whoops and hollers. "And when that day comes—when that day has come and gone, there'll be people left alive on this earth—gay people and straight people, men and women, black and white—who will hear the story that once there was a terrible disease in this country and all over the world, and that a brave group of people stood up and fought, and in some cases, gave their lives so that other people might live and be free.[20]

28

AMERICAN PSYCHO

In June of 1994, Bob Krasnow left Elektra due to a major corporate shakeup by The Warner Music Group, which owned the label.[1] It was a huge loss to the industry, and an even bigger one for me. The new chairperson was Sylvia Rhone. Once she took over, I didn't have that warm feeling working at Elektra that I had when Bob was there. I just said to myself, "I gotta get out of here."

The only other place I knew of that had the same prestigious roster as Elektra, was Geffen. In late 1996, I met once again with the president of Geffen, Ed Rosenblatt, and he offered me back my A&R position at the label.

Did I love the idea of going back there? In theory, yes—I was a big fan of Ed's, but the prospect wasn't a huge thrill. Geffen is located in Los Angeles and because I didn't drive, I didn't swim, and I wasn't going to move out there, it meant returning to the satellite office here in the city, which was not ideal. Many of the Geffen A&R executives in L.A. were pitted against each other. The egos were so fucking big and with me going back into the New York office, I could easily be forgotten. But I wasn't going to let any of that get to me. I wasn't looking to compete; I just wanted to do an awesome job.

Like Elektra, Geffen was a major label that operated as a boutique label. The A&R execs were very specific about their signings. There was never anything "run of the mill" about that label. They only signed the crème de la crème—artists like Cher, Sonic Youth, Nirvana, Guns N' Roses, and White Zombie.

✹   ✹   ✹

I was interested in the Misfits as early as 1983, when they played CBGB's. At that point, in 1997 when I signed them, the album they would be recording would be their first on a major label. It would also be the first without their front man, Glenn Danzig. The landscape was seriously changing for them. They had to get a new singer and it was very hard to compete with Danzig—he was a founding member with Jerry Only and, as a singer, a true original.

They ended up going with a young musician and singer who looked the part, named Michael Graves. The band was now Michael, Jerry Only on bass, his brother Doyle on guitar, and drummer, Dr. Chud.

When I heard their new songs, I thought they were killer! They were all still inspired by horror movies, but I actually thought of the band as a pop band—not in the Top 40 pop band way, but their songs were sing-alongs and easy to remember.

The album was called *American Psycho*. It was produced by my dear friend Daniel Rey. Daniel had worked with the Ramones and Iggy Pop, and was a member of the band, The Masters of Reality, as well as being in the first band I ever signed, Shrapnel. Andy Wallace mixed the album and we hired him once again because of the previous work he had done for Slayer. The original painting on the album cover was by Basil Gogos, whose gorgeous renditions of such classic horror stars as Bela Lugosi and Lon Chaney graced the covers of *Famous Monsters of Filmland*.

Initially, I think it sold about fifty thousand units, but honestly, the success (or non-success) of my records at Geffen had more to do with me being in a satellite office. I wasn't in everybody's face and the A&R people in the main office received preference.

It was clear that the staff wasn't making *American Psycho* a top priority, and I could already feel they weren't going to make a second studio album with the band. Geffen wasn't supporting any of my projects financially so I decided to leave the label once again.

Before I left Geffen, I went with the Misfits on their first European tour. It was also the first time I met Drew Stone. Drew managed a small band called Subzero. He had asked the Misfits' Jerry Only if Subzero could join them on tour, and Jerry agreed. All I remember about that tour was a lot of beer drinking and fighting. I was the one in most of those fights because once I started drinking, I turned into a bit of a fun-loving prick. Nonetheless, it was a very fortuitous thing that I met Drew on this tour.

29

PRISON MATES

In 1997, I started corresponding with inmates in state prisons in Washington and Louisiana. There was a pen pal site for prisoners and I was drawn to it because I was intrigued by the potential sexual aspect of it, like I always was in my previous "relationships." I liked that it was from a distance, too. I have always felt more comfortable with distance.

One day, I saw a picture of a young man, and I thought, I'm gonna be his pen pal! Not only did we end up writing to each other, but I went to visit him in prison.

His name was Marty. He was in his late twenties and was in prison at Airway Heights Corrections Center, in Washington State. He had been there since he was seventeen, on a first-degree assault charge. His friend had shot someone seven times while Marty was in the same room. He was arrested under the Washington State Accomplice Law and got seventeen years in prison, serving fifteen. He had been in the wrong place at the wrong time.

When I went to visit him at Airway Heights, I was nervous and excited to make the trip. It was clear after a few minutes of talking with him that this was going to turn into some kind of relationship. I wrote to him every week, sending postcards and letters, and we talked on the phone at least once or twice a week. I knew he wasn't gay, but there was deep caring and warmth in our connection—it became very intimate. We were important to each other—filling a sense of loneliness we each had. Marty is a wonderful guy. Since his release, he's gotten married and had two kids, and we've stayed close through it all. It's kind of odd how I always ended up keeping these long-term friendships with men I have met over the years, even if they weren't romantic.

I also started corresponding with another prisoner named Frank, and I was amazed by how handsome he was. He had been convicted of the murder of a deputy, which he insisted he did not commit. Frank and his brother had been in jail in West Carroll Parish Detention Center on a sixty-day sentence for simple assault (he was in a fistfight), when a friend of theirs—who was in a crazed state of mind—arrived at the detention center to aid in their escape. He said Frank and his brother were his only friends. However, in the process, Frank's friend shot and killed the deputy who was on duty. Frank snatched the gun from his friend because the guy was in a psychotic state and had said he planned to kill his father and girlfriend. At some point, Frank and his brother took the friend to some nearby woods, where he fell asleep. Frank and his brother pretended to sleep as well, but didn't, instead they gathered up all of the friend's guns and hid them. Then Frank and his brother went to turn themselves in, because they had left the jail illegally.

Unfortunately, the authorities had seen Frank with the gun after he had taken it from his friend and put him and his brother on trial for murder. They did this even though the police knew Frank and his brother weren't the culprits, but that it was their friend who killed the deputy. Because Frank couldn't afford a good attorney, he and his brother were convicted and given the death penalty, even though they were innocent. He ended up spending two decades in solitary confinement. Turns out the attorney who prosecuted Frank was convicted of ethics charges in 1998.

Frank is now incarcerated in Louisiana State Penitentiary, known as "Angola" after the plantation that originally occupied that territory. It is the largest maximum security prison in the U.S. and, like San Quentin, one of the most dangerous. You didn't go there for committing petty offenses, that's for sure.

Frank and I talked all the time on the phone; the first time I went to visit him was on July 4, 2002. I went to New Orleans and made my way to the Batiste Bus Line, located at the corner of Jackson & Claiborne streets, in the A-1 Appliance parking lot. I had to be there at 7:30 a.m. for an 8 a.m. departure. The bus ride was over two-and-a-half hours long. It was 100 degrees outside and the air conditioner on the bus had a mind of its own, going on and off all the way to Angola.

Most of the women on the bus were black. When I boarded, one of them looked at me and said, "Honey! Do you know where you're goin'?" I snapped my fingers very "gayly" and said, "I'm goin' to see my husband!"

I sat in a seat near the front and noticed an older woman sitting across from the driver. She was also the only white woman on the bus, which I thought was a little curious. About an hour into the trip, we turned into a rest stop and everyone got off to use the restroom and get some food. As I walked down the steps of the bus, I looked at the woman in the front seat, and asked her, "Would you like anything to eat or drink? I can get something for you."

"No thank you," she said. "That's very nice of you, but I do this trip every week and I bring my own food."

I nodded and smiled and went off to get something to eat, thinking in my restless mind—Do I *know* that woman?

After I got some chips and a sandwich, I returned and ended up sitting in the seat behind the woman. She turned around and looked at me.

"I guess you're not from New Orleans, are you?"

"I am not," I said.

"Would you like to come sit next to me up here?" she offered.

"Sure!"

We started talking about who she was going to visit at Angola and I soon learned she was Sister Helen Prejean. I had seen the movie[1] about her, based on her book, *Dead Man Walking*.[2] I couldn't believe I was sitting next to her!

She was very quiet and soft spoken. She told me how she had become a nun in 1957 at the age of eighteen when she joined the Sisters of St. Joseph of Medaille (now known as the Congregation of St. Joseph). To my mind, she was a living saint.

> Sister Helen began her prison ministry in 1981 when she dedicated her life to the poor of New Orleans. While living in the St. Thomas housing project, she became pen pals with Patrick Sonnier, the convicted killer of two teenagers, sentenced to die in the electric chair of Louisiana's Angola State Prison. . . . Upon Sonnier's request, Sister Helen repeatedly visited him as his spiritual advisor. In doing so, her eyes were opened to the Louisiana execution process.[3]

When we arrived at the penitentiary, a small van picked us up to drop us at the area where the prisoners resided. I said goodbye to Sister Helen but I saw her around the grounds throughout the afternoon, visiting many of the prisoners.

Before seeing the inmates, we were guided to a "check-in" area, where we had to empty our pockets of all of our personal belongings: keys, money, wallet—everything—and put it all into a locker, which we closed with a key that we hung around our wrists. After we finished, we walked down a hallway through enormous steel doors, which were slammed shut with a bolt after we passed through. The sound of the bolt was deafening, and jolted me. I looked back at it with worry. We were then led into the community room, where I waited to meet Frank.

When I saw him, I was exhilarated. It was our first time seeing each other after a year of writing letters. He was close to six feet tall with dark hair and he was tan from lifting weights out in the sun. I was only allowed to give him a hug, and only *one* hug at that. It felt very special.

That whole day we sat and played cards and talked. Then I said, "Frank, can I keep these cards when I leave so I can remember today?" Except what I actually wanted was his T-shirt. He had an opened button-down shirt with a T-shirt underneath, but getting that out of the prison without getting caught, well, *that* was another story.

"Wait here," he said. "I'm going to the bathroom to take off my shirt and leave it in there. Then you can go in and put it on underneath your own shirt."

We could have gotten into a lot of trouble if we got caught. They would have likely put Frank back into solitary confinement, and those small cells are designed to drive you stir-crazy.

Luckily, we weren't caught, and I was able to leave with a little bit of Frank. We continue to write to each other to this day, and we talk on the phone weekly. His lawyer is trying to get his sentence overturned as Frank was not the one who pulled the trigger. Meanwhile, his prison term has been reduced and he is no longer on death row—but is now serving life while a new team of lawyers work to secure his release.

30

NO MORE MR. RECORD EXECUTIVE

During 1999, I met a number of times with Chris Blackwell, the founder of Island Records, who was starting a new company called Palm Pictures. I met with him about possibly joining their A&R department. As the deal was being considered, my friend Mina Caputo asked me if I wanted to be involved with her first solo project.

For the life of me, I don't really know when I met Mina, but I believe it was around 1993. All I know is that the moment we met, we both knew that it was a friendship that would last for the rest of our lives. Mina was still Keith at that point. She did not start transitioning until a few years later and through it all, she continues to be that charming, creative, talented human being.

Mina has been the front person and lyricist for Life of Agony since that band's inception. Her live performances are electric, and she has that wildly charismatic, Jim Morrison quality on stage.

Around 1997, while Mina was still Keith, he took a break from the band and, in 1998, decided he wanted to make a solo album. Given my experience as an A&R executive—not to mention being his friend—he wanted my involvement, so I took on the job of executive producer. After a few conversations, we decided we wanted the album to come from a traditional, storytelling perspective, with a lot of mood and dark atmosphere.

We started researching producers and we looked on the Billboard charts and the name Jared Kotler jumped out at us. He had a number-one hit single with "Sex and Candy" by the band Marcy Playground. We called him at his recording studio, The Orchard House, in Kings Point, New York, located on the grounds of a horse ranch estate. The production of his current record interested us, and we set up a meeting with him to discuss Keith's album. In conversation, Jared came across as smart and unconventional, which made us feel he just might be the right person to make this record for us.

We were excited about the recording. Keith had a ton of songs which we narrowed down to twelve that we knew were going to tell an inspiring story. From the get-go, I thought we had this mini-masterpiece on our hands. But I didn't want to get too excited too quickly. Yet, as an A&R executive, I know when something is going to be magical. That album had the makings of magic.

Before long, we were in Jared's Long Island studio, laying down some basic tracks. There were vintage Persian rugs on the floor, which kept the sound in the room warm and ambient. It was the beginning of a phenomenal experience.

The songs were amazing and Jared brought in brilliant musicians such as Craig Ross, guitarist and longtime associate of Lenny Kravitz; Gerry Leonard, who played guitar with David Bowie—and was personally chosen by Bowie to play on his last tour; the great drummer, Steven Wolf; and the fabulous Jack Daley on bass; as well as many other highly respected session players.

We planned to hire Mike Shipley to mix the album after we finished laying down all the tracks with Jared. Mike was a superstar engineer,[1] having worked with the Sex Pistols and Queen early in his career, and later, with various artists, most notably Tom Petty and the Heartbreakers and Def Leppard. I didn't even know if we could afford him, because his fee was way up in the stratosphere. But what I do remember is that any time I needed money, I went to the Business Affairs department at Roadrunner Records, the label releasing the album. I would ask for another $10,000—another $20,000—another $30,000—and believe it or not, we got all the money. We ended up spending nearly $250,000 on this record that no one at Roadrunner understood or even cared about.

Roadrunner is a hard rock, heavy metal label and had released three Life of Agony albums: *River Runs Red, Ugly, and Soul Searching Sun.* But Keith's solo record was very different. It had a John Lennon quality, something Roadrunner was not at all known for. We were very proud of the album and yet I wound up having many arguments with Business Affairs and the A&R department about the final results.

We went out to Los Angeles to have the record mixed by Shipley. I always preferred to go to the studio where the mixing engineer worked, because they were familiar with the room and knew how to get the biggest and best sounds of what was just laid down on tape. Mike was a sweetheart, despite the fact that he never wanted us in the studio looking over his shoulder while he was mixing. We were somewhat amused but never fought him on this, because we knew we were going to get back a worldclass, brilliantly mixed album.

When we arrived at the studio, the first person we ran into was Eminem, which stopped us dead in our tracks. Keith extended his hand and said hello. I just stood there, frozen. We knew that Dr. Dre was producing his album, although we never got a chance to meet him. We heard Marilyn Manson was in the next studio doing mixing work as well. There was a strong, creative energy throughout each of the studios, coming out of the work Mike and all those major artists were doing. In that moment, we *knew* we were in the right place.

The first day we arrived in L.A., we stayed at the Beverly Garland Holiday Inn in Burbank. The hotel was named after the actress from *My Three Sons*—such a hoot! Very camp! However, we ended up moving the following day to West Hollywood to be closer to the studio and all the action. We wanted to stay at The Standard on Sunset Boulevard because we knew the rooms were furnished with silver leather bean bag chairs, and the curtains were covered with the famous Andy Warhol flower prints. The room we were in was modern, but definitely a throwback to the sixties.

We also brought a book on the teachings of the Sufi, Islamic scholar and theologian, Rumi. His words guided us throughout our entire journey. The book we carried with us was *The Essential Rumi* and we held it close throughout the entire trip because we felt it gave us the spiritual guidance we were looking for. Every day, we opened it to a new page and read a few words of wisdom for the day, such as "Shine like the universe is yours."

One night, Keith and I rented a vintage Cadillac convertible to celebrate. We bought a couple bottles of champagne and we both dropped a hit of ecstasy. Even before we left the hotel, we were laughing and screaming while Keith painted his toenails. We knew we wanted to go for a late-night drive, so we took the car and drove up to the Hollywood sign on Mount Lee in the Hollywood Hills. On the way there, we went up Mulholland Drive to the area where the very rich live. We were feeling very "David Lynch." We laughed and sang as the ecstasy kicked in. I soon noticed a security guard a few feet up the hill, so I told Keith to put out his joint and hide the champagne bottles under the seat. Of course, when security stopped us, we apologized, said we took a wrong turn, that we were from New York and didn't know where we were going. The guard very sternly let us know we had to exit the area immediately.

A few days later, when we were heading back to New York City, I reached out to the photographer Edward Mapplethorpe, to shoot the front cover of the album. Edward did a session with Keith at the beach. It was the dead of winter. All Keith had on was white gauze and it was twenty degrees out. I also reached out to Carol Friedman, who shot exquisite studios photographs of Keith.

Eventually, Roadrunner let us know they weren't releasing the album in the United States. We were completely thrown! The album was a work of art, although certainly not the type of recording that Roadrunner had in its catalogue. It was released in Germany and Japan, the Netherlands, and the UK, but we were very disappointed by the label's overall lack of support.

A number of years later, Keith transitioned to Mina. It has been so inspirational to see my dear friend blossom and truly become her authentic self. In many of our conversations about her transitioning, we were concerned about the possible negative effect on her career and on Life of Agony. However, what happened was the exact opposite—she was accepted with love and acclaim by all her fans. We've had many intimate conversations during this self-liberating process, and I have found my dear friend to be very brave and courageous. Mina has always been a person about truth and honesty and, as a result, people respond to her with nothing but love.

❈   ❈   ❈

Thankfully, the job at Palm Pictures came through and I started there in 2000. Palm Pictures is an entertainment company that acquires and distributes both film and music.

While I was there, the first band I signed was Speedealer. They were from Dallas, Texas, and were a noisy bunch—they made a mighty racket—and I adored every waking moment of them. I contacted Jason Newsted from Metallica to produce their album and I loved how he unified their sound yet allowed them to still steam roll through all of the songs with a kick-ass intensity. It was called *Second Sight*, and was just fantastic.

After I brought in Speedealer, Palm's business affairs office began assigning bands to me they had already brought onto the label. One of those bands was Fozzy, headed by the famed wrestler Chris Jericho and included his infamous sidekick, Rich Ward, of Stuck Mojo—pioneers of rap-metal. At some point they wanted to name the band "Fozzy Osbourne," but Sharon Osbourne nixed that immediately.

Because Chris was a highly successful wrestler at the time, there was a real buzz about their self-titled debut album, which came out in 2000 on the Palm and Megaforce labels. Unfortunately, it failed to make the Billboard charts. Since that debut, the band has released seven albums and continue to tour worldwide, killin' it wherever they go.

Another one of the bands assigned to me was Local H. Local H was formed by guitarist and vocalist, Scott Lucas, and drummer, Joe Daniels, both from Zion, Illinois. Though Scott has remained the central figure in the duo, there has been an ever-changing cast of drummers—except for Brian St. Clair, who played in Local H the longest, from 1999–2013.

> The duo that turned "keep it copacetic" into a primal anthem revive Nirvana's brand of anarchic rock, replete with sly slacker lyrics, screeching slogans ("Hands on the Bible!"), and feedback-drenched hidden tracks. Brian St. Clair can't provide the bottom-heavy kick of old drummer Joe Daniels, but guests like Queens of the Stone Age's Josh Homme and the Misfits' Jerry Only complete Scott Lucas' (guitar, bass, vocals) noisy symphony.[2]

We grabbed Jack Douglas[3] to produce, because we loved his work with John Lennon and Aerosmith. The album, titled *Here Comes The Zoo*, did pretty well, making it to number thirteen on Billboard's Top Independent Album chart.

✿   ✿   ✿

A couple months after working on the recording of *Here Comes the Zoo*, I was at home making some tea. While I waited for the water to boil, I went out onto my terrace to enjoy what looked like a glorious morning. I live on 17th Street in Chelsea and my balcony faces south. I have a clear shot view of downtown New York City and the World Trade Center.

As I was out there, I suddenly heard my neighbor, Cathy, scream. I share the terrace with her, so I leaned over the partition to look into her apartment.

"Cathy! "Is everything okay?"

She ran out.

"Michael! *Look!*"

I turned around. I couldn't believe what I was seeing.

"Wait a minute," I gasped. "Are the Twin Towers . . . on fire?" My eyes stopped cold, in shock.

Seventeenth street had been my home for the last six years, and the constant view from my terrace was of the magnificent city skyline.

"I think an airplane crashed into the World Trade Center!" Cathy said.

I saw huge clouds of smoke billowing up from the force of whatever was happening, whatever was hitting the World Trade Center. I couldn't believe what I was seeing. I ran back inside to turn on CNN, and Cathy came racing over. She left my front door open and my neighbors on the entire 15th floor started streaming into the apartment. We congregated on my terrace and in front of the television. We all watched in horror. CNN finally said that New York City was under attack. We didn't know what to think—or do.

Meanwhile, the second airplane hadn't struck yet, but it did within minutes. Then we started to see people throwing themselves out of the World Trade Center windows. Everyone went completely silent. It was the most horrible thing we ever witnessed in our lives. The next six months I had to keep my windows closed because whenever the smoke blew north, I was hit with "an acrid burning type smell. A mixture of vaporized burnt plastic, electronics, burnt paper, wood, steel and concrete, jet fuel, ozone and a sickly sweet edge and lot of very old re-awakened NYC dust. . . . The intense heat and burning produced by the airplane fuel and the mixture of all those synthetic (and organic) materials, from the tons of electronics produced some noxious toxic gases."[4] Those sickening smells always brought back the terror of that day.

The city took a long time to recover and it still hasn't in many ways. One of the first realities from the attack that I came across was when I flew to Paris about a month later. I went there to attend an exhibition of my photographs. There were only five or six people on that 747—an airplane that could hold over four hundred passengers—but there were only a handful. It was eerie.

※　　※　　※

During this time while I was still at Palm, I started drinking and drugging again. It was growing into a huge problem. I was also very interested in signing a charismatic singer-songwriter named Guy Forsyth, but the Palm Pictures staff didn't agree with me. The writing was on the wall. The executives at the label didn't give a damn about any of the artists I was looking to sign. However, that wasn't the primary reason I finally left.

I looked around at the music business, and there seemed to be the beginning of a massive shift. Within the emerging online world of the internet and personal computers in the nineties, music fans and professionals were now illegally file-sharing and downloading music on a huge scale. There was no official monitoring over that process from the technology or music industries. Retail chains, such as Tower Records and Virgin Megastores, started facing bankruptcies and possible closures. Recording artists were facing enormous losses in royalty earnings. The changes facing the music industry were colossal.

I had worked through unprecedented times in the business. But that was all changing. After twenty-four years of loving my job, developing artists, having massive successes and a few failures, I decided this wasn't the place for me anymore. Between the unforeseen changes in the way music was now being developed and distributed, and the substance abuse overwhelming me, I was beginning to fall apart again.

❊   ❊   ❊

After I left Palm, I became even more focused on my photography. One of the early portraits I took was of Hilly Kristal, famed owner of CBGB's. Hilly was basically a surrogate father to all of us teens taking refuge at CBs. It became our home away from home. He welcomed us all—though he often reminded us if he caught us with alcohol in our hands, we would be banned for a few weeks. Hilly was one of the first club owners to promote to the exploding punk rock music scene coming out of both the U.S. and Britain, and through it all, he gave us a sense of family.

When Hilly closed the club in 2006, he opened a place on St. Mark's called CBGB Shoppe, and it definitely had the atmosphere of a Trash & Vaudeville store. On one side of the shop was a mural-sized photo of the front of CBGB's, and on the opposite wall was a mural-sized photo of the stage.

Hilly was very ill. He was going through chemotherapy for lung cancer and he seemed pretty delicate and was very thin. When I arrived to take his picture, I asked him if he wanted me to come another day.

"No, let's do it," he insisted.

I shot the photograph of him in front of each of the murals. He was very generous with this time, the afternoon went really well, and his photo[5] came out beautifully. Unfortunately, he died the following August.[6]

Those years—the late seventies and early eighties—when Hilly ran CBs, were vibrant and exceptional. There was an unstoppable energy from everyone in the music community. New York will never be the same as so many of those souls are now angels and ghosts.

✤　✤　✤

Not long after I took Hilly's portrait, I went to New Orleans to see the catastrophic aftermath of Hurricane Katrina, which hit in 2005. I wanted to make sure my New Orleans friends—among them George Dureau, Sean Yseult and Philip and Kate—were safe.

With my friend J, from White Zombie, we drove to the Lower Ninth Ward to visit the devastation—it was horrifying to see. Home after home, block after block, roofs blown off, houses leveled to the ground, like a massive cement roller just ran over everything and wiped it all out. An estimated "80 percent of New Orleans and large portions of nearby parishes became flooded, and the floodwaters did not recede for weeks."[7]

As we wandered the flattened-out streets, we saw codes written by FEMA on the front of many of the houses. The codes were called "Katrina Crosses," which "summarized the hazards and horrors found within,"[8] such as how many people had been found alive or dead.

J and I also came across Fats Domino's house, which had been a landmark in the Lower Ninth Ward since the sixties.

Many feared that Fats was dead—one fan even spray-painted a message on his home: "RIP Fats. You will be missed." But later that day, CNN reported that he had been rescued by a coast guard helicopter on 1 September 2005.[9]

It was both his home and his publishing office and had been flooded, destroyed and abandoned. We entered through an open door on the side. The place had basically been gutted. We stood there for a moment just quietly looking around. We saw some little fleur-de-lis–shaped mirrors by the back bar and, from the devastation, a bunch of them had fallen onto the floor. They were so beautiful, I picked one up and stuck it in my pocket as a memento. We climbed up the stairs to the second floor and came across Fats' famous Cadillac sofa. It had been wiped out by the hurricane, although part of it was still intact, including the license plates.

✿　　✿　　✿

When I returned to New York, I couldn't stop feeling that I had to get hold of my drinking and drugging. The overwhelming amount I was consuming was beginning to destroy me, both physically and mentally. There I was—approaching the age of fifty—facing a life and death struggle, again.

31

SOBER NOT SOBER

After I left Hazelden, I was sober for eight years. I was what they call a "dry drunk." I didn't go to meetings—I only went to a few of the men's groups I had been urged to attend. I was still suffering "king baby syndrome."[1] I was going to show them I didn't need to drink. I was still arrogant.

Sometime in 1999, someone asked me if I wanted a beer and I said, "Yes." That was it. Those years—from the age of forty until I walked into a recovery room at age forty-seven—were the worst of my life.

I was drinking all the time, which meant I was taking my HIV meds with hard alcohol and beer. To fall asleep at night I would down a Budweiser, a Klonopin, and some Nyquil. When I got up in the morning, I was so thick-headed, so groggy, I wasn't able to think straight for hours.

Then very late one night, around 3 a.m., I was walking along Christopher Street and I saw this gorgeous blond man standing there. I edged up close to him.

"I have crack in my pocket," I whispered. "Would you like to come home with me?"

"No thanks, he said. "I'm a police officer and you're under arrest."

I was furious!

"What the hell!" I screamed. Then I pulled my dick out and pissed all over his leg. I was so angry. He grabbed me by my collar, whipped me around, threw me up against an unmarked van, handcuffed me, and brought me to a holding pen on 10th Street. They fingerprinted me and everything.

I had to call Danny Fields in the morning to get me out. But when I was released, it just started all over again.

There were times when I wound up in St. Vincent's Hospital because I had gone into a cocaine psychosis. When that happened, my mind always raced to the fear that I would jump off my terrace, or that I was simply going to die some other way. Many times I was hooked up to IVs and monitors in the hospital to make sure I hadn't damaged my heart.

There was one time when I ended up in New Orleans, and I have no idea how that happened. I don't remember getting on an airplane or in a taxi. I don't how or why the airline authorities even allowed me on the plane, but the next thing I knew, I was in the worst neighborhood of New Orleans. I wound up in the back of a dilapidated house, smoking crack with some girl.

When the other addicts in the crack house realized I had no more money, they literally kicked my ass out onto the street. I *did* have some extra cash, but because I knew I was wandering in a very bad area, I hid it in my sock.

I was so fucked up that moments after they threw me out, I spotted a cute couple on the street and immediately tried to pick them up. They invited me to some flea-bitten motel and the next thing I knew, they were robbing me of everything, including the money in my sock. They left me with just my boxer shorts on and my sneakers.

Enraged, I stormed out of the motel and started marching down the street, trying to get back to *somewhere*. A cop car suddenly pulled up next to me and one of the policemen opened the window:

"Sir, do you have I.D.?" he asked.

I looked at them incredulously, and because I was so high and full of myself, I said: "Do I *look* like I have fucking I.D.? I just got *robbed!*"

They literally laughed in my face.

"You're not from this neighborhood, are you?"

"No, I'm from New York City!"

"Get in the car and we'll drive you to where you're staying."

Except I heard it as they were going to drive me home to New York.

"Oh, Officer, you're going to drive me *home*?"

"Sir," he said, rolling his eyes. "Do you have an address here in New Orleans or not?"

"Oh, okay, yes—um . . . Felicity Street."

They drove me to my friend's house on Felicity Street and, apparently, there was a party going on. As the cop car approached, everyone at the party got real quiet because they thought the cops were there to shut them down. I fell out of the back seat of the police car with just my underwear and my sneakers on and when they all saw me, somebody shouted: "Wait a minute! *Is that Alago?*"

I waved and laughed. I was so high. The police pulled away and everyone was laughing their heads off. Then, I passed out, right on the ground.

Those were the kinds of things that were happening all the time during those years from forty to forty-seven. It felt like it was okay, that it was the norm. I was a walking zombie.

When you're in the throes of heavy addiction you just do what you want, when you want, and you don't consider the consequences.

✿   ✿   ✿

I first met Linda Stein when I was in my early twenties. We became close and stayed connected over the years. She was Danny Fields' business partner and best friend for nearly four decades. In the late seventies and early eighties, she and Danny managed the Ramones.

> [Linda] stormed her way up from middle-class Riverdale to become something of a star herself. In 1975, she'd taken one look at the Ramones, decided they were the future of rock, and helped launch their incendiary ascent. A fixture at CBGB, the Mudd Club, and Studio 54, she leveraged her friendships in the eighties to become the first and greatest celebrity real-estate broker, selling to Madonna, Sting, Donna Karan, Bruce Willis and Demi Moore, and Billy Joel and Christie Brinkley.[2]

Linda made a fortune in real estate. She was known as the "realtor to the stars" and had been married to Seymour Stein, president of Sire Records.

Danny and I would often go to her home for Sunday dinner. It was always warm and celebratory with lots of laughs. It was like family.

[It] was 1973 and [Danny] was the editor of *16* magazine—"a teenybopper fan mag"—and he was desperate to get Elton John in its pages. Mr. Fields knew the Steins were friends with the musician, so he printed an agency photo of Linda Stein and Mr. John, captioning Ms. Stein as a "glamorous New York socialite." "That got me on her party list and we became good friends," Mr. Fields says.[3]

✿   ✿   ✿

In early October of 2007, I went up to a friend's place in Woodstock with some music business people for the weekend. It was a beautiful day and there were a lot of families and children—all jumping in and out of the pool.

But my two crazy friends and I, we ended up staying in the kitchen snorting coke, snorting coke, and snorting more coke. At one point, we needed more liquor so we drove to the store, got another case of champagne and continued drinking and snorting all day long.

Later, in the evening, everybody was heading off to bed—all the kids and their parents. The house quieted down as everyone feel asleep, but I found I couldn't. I kept tossing and turning, and it infuriated me. I started knocking on everyone's bedroom doors to see if anyone had Valium. No one did, and I started to freak out. That was Friday, October 19.

The next day, everyone was up and rested, but I was completely wiped out. I hadn't been able to sleep at all and I was so wired, my hands were shaking and sweating.

I decided to walk to the Greyhound bus station. When I got back home to my apartment in Chelsea, I was still hyper and couldn't come down from all the drugs. I felt like I was having a heart attack. I had no idea what to do, so I paced back and forth, back and forth in my living room. Then I passed out on the sofa.

When I woke up the following morning, on Sunday, the 21st and looked around, I decided to take a shower. I have no clear idea about the next few moments—I have no memory of speaking to anyone that morning. Was it a moment of grace? Was it a white light experience? I have no idea. But after I got out of the shower, I got dressed and walked downtown to a twelve-step meeting in the Village. I'd heard about the place but had never been there before. Somehow I knew there was a meeting beginning at 2:30 that afternoon.

When I arrived, I sat down in one of the chairs in the main room. There was a lovely man who took the seat next to me. I learned during the course of the meeting, that he had twenty-five years clean and sober. He was very comforting and said to me, "Everything will be okay as long as you keep coming back, one day at a time."

I paid attention to his kind words, which began to resonate with me. This was the beginning of a major turning point in my life. I started going to meetings every morning.

About eight days later, on October 29, I called Linda Stein.

"Linda!"

"Hello, dear!" she said. "How are you?"

"I'm sure you're going to be very happy when I tell you, I'm finally serious about getting sober."

"*Tatala!*" she cried. "This is the best news I ever heard! Are you hitting the Village meeting?"

"I am!"

"Wonderful! Tomorrow I want to take you out for a meal and we'll talk." We made plans to meet the following evening.

Early the next morning, I was in the shower when I heard the telephone ringing off the hook. I jumped out, grabbed a towel, and picked up the phone. It was Mandy Stein, Linda's daughter, and she was screaming and crying.

"Mom is dead!" she cried. "I think Mom was killed! I don't have any details! But she's dead! Michael! Michael! How are we going to tell Danny?!"

I went into a state of shock. My brain was going numb; I didn't know what to think. I was supposed to have had dinner with Linda that night.

I pulled myself together as fast as I could.

"Are you okay, Mandy?

"I don't know!" she screamed back. "But we have to tell Danny!"

"Okay," I said. "Give me your number. I need to go over to Danny's and tell him this in person."

Mandy hung up. She was heading to the police station.

A woman who helped pioneer the punk music scene, influenced the careers of Madonna and the Ramones and went on to become known as a real estate agent to the stars was found bludgeoned to death Tuesday night in her apartment at 965 Fifth Avenue, the police said.[4]

I called Danny. He was very groggy when he picked up the phone.

"I need to come over to your place immediately," I said. "There's something important I have to tell you."

He was really upset at me for waking him up so early in the morning. "*What?*"

I could tell he hadn't slept much. He told me a trick was there.

"Danny—get rid of the trick right now!" I said.

"Can't you just call me later?"

"Danny!" I shouted. "This is very important! Please get up now!"

He was still really annoyed with me.

"Okay, Danny, I'm coming to your house now—I have the keys. And I'm really sorry to have to tell you this on the phone—Linda is dead."

"*What? What do you mean?!*"

"I think she was killed."

He started getting hysterical. I told him that I would be there in fifteen minutes. I hung up the phone, threw on some clothes, grabbed the keys, ran over to his apartment, and let myself in. I saw the trick was still there. I picked up his jeans from the floor and threw them at him.

"*Get the fuck out!*"

Then I turned to Danny.

"Get in the shower and clean yourself up."

The phone started ringing like mad. I picked it up.

"Hi, is this Danny Fields' residence?" the voice on the line said.

"Yes. Who am I speaking to?"

"This is Sandy Kenyon from *Eyewitness News*. May I speak with Mr. Fields?"

"No, actually. But I'm taking down names and numbers and we will be happy to get back to you. We just got this news."

I must've taken tons of calls that day but it was awhile before we could handle them. We were still in shock and waiting to hear what happened. Finally, Danny called Mandy.

> Mrs. Stein, who lived alone in Manhattan, was beaten to death but police say there were no signs of a break-in or robbery and cannot find any motive for the killing . . . [h]er body was found on Tuesday by her daughter but the cause of death was not confirmed until an autopsy yesterday.[5]

Later in the afternoon, I ended up going to one of my meetings when a very strange thing happened. When the meeting ended, and I walked out to head back to Danny's, a person from the *New York Post* suddenly approached me. Granted I was still in a daze—between what had happened to Linda and that I had only been sober for eight days—but it seemed very odd to me that the press knew where I was.

> The day before Stein was found bludgeoned to death in her Fifth Avenue living room, she made plans by phone to attend an Alcoholics Anonymous meeting with Michael Alago, a former record executive she knew from her days as co-manager of the Ramones.[6]

About two days later, the police called me. They wanted to talk to me about Linda's murder, and they gave me two choices: "You can either come meet with us up here at the precinct, or we can meet with you at your home. Pick one."

Apparently, my name was one of the last ones on Linda's phone—which makes sense because we had made plans for dinner the following night, although the police had no knowledge of that.

They showed up within the hour at my apartment. They wanted to know how long I had known Linda, when was the last time I actually saw her, when was the last time I was at her home, and mostly, why was my name one of the last names on her phone.

I explained that we had been friends for a long time, that we had met at CBGB's in the late seventies, and that she had planned to take me out to dinner to celebrate my new sobriety.

The personal assistant of Linda S. Stein, who had managed the Ramones and was a real estate agent for celebrities, was convicted on Tuesday of second-degree murder in the bludgeoning death of Ms. Stein in October 2007.[7]

32

MEMPHIS BLUES

In 2008, I received a conference call from Cyndi Lauper and her manager, Lisa Barbaris.[1]

"Hi, Michael! I need help!" Cyndi said, and because my mind was so wrapped up in my recovery, I said to her, "Oh, Cyndi! I didn't know you drank!"

"Michael! I *don't* drink! I need help making an album!"

She wanted to make a dance record, and I was excited to help her with it. It was called *Bring Ya to the Brink* and was released in May of that year.

I had originally met Cyndi back in 1980, when she was still with her band Blue Angel and I was the booking agent at The Ritz. I adored her and was so touched when she contacted me to work not only on *Bring Ya to the Brink* but also, two years later—on a new project.

I got that call from her in early 2010, and she said she wanted to do something totally different.

"I want to make a blues album."

I smiled, because I knew Cyn was always up for an adventure but—*a blues album?*

"Well, Michael, I know you know how to make a heavy metal record, but have you ever made a blues album before?"

"No," I replied. "Have *you* ever made a blues album?

"Well . . . no," she said.

"Then we're on an even playing field."

We had a bit of a laugh.

I was very interested in the project. I have tremendous respect for Cyndi as an artist and, although we were heading into new territory, I had a good feeling about it.

The following week, I went to her home on the Upper West Side and we sat in her kitchen, ate Chinese food, and pulled out her blues archives. As Cyndi recalls it: "We listened to hours and hours of music for many weeks until we came up with the list of songs that I eventually recorded for the album. We had a great time, and we had an easy time connecting to each other."[2]

Cyndi was thinking of signing with an independent label called Downtown Records. The head of Downtown was an executive named Josh Deutsch, and he suggested Scott Bomar[3] to produce the album.

I decided to do some research on Scott. He was a thirty-six-year-old musician, composer, and producer who had been working for years on the Memphis music scene. He had deep connections with all the local musicians, including Al Green's band, Isaac Hayes' band, and every major blues artist you could think of, and it excited us beyond words.

We had an initial meeting with Scott and cut two songs with him to see if he got a sense of the sound we were looking for. It worked out brilliantly. We went down to Memphis to make the record in Scott's studio, Electraphonic Recording.

It was a thrill and delight when we started the album. Not long after we arrived, Cyndi said to Scott, "You know, I love Ann Peebles, because I adore that song, 'I Can't Stand the Rain.' Do you have any contact with her?"

Scott said she lived around the corner.

"Do you want me to call her up?" he asked with a sly smile and a wink.

Cyndi's eyes opened wide and everybody had a good laugh. They called her and she came over. She ended up singing on the track, "Rollin' and Tumblin'."

We were also very fond of Jonny Lang,[4] who, when he was originally signed to A&M Records, was a teenage guitar prodigy. He is a world-class musician and, luckily, we were able to get him to perform on the tracks "How Blue Can You Get?" and "Crossroads." Scott also suggested Charlie Musselwhite,[5] a renowned harmonica player and band leader whom we featured on the tracks, "Down Don't Bother Me" and "Just Your Fool." Charlie is often referred to as the "white bluesman" and was the inspiration for Dan Akroyd's character in the 1980 film *The Blues Brothers*.

BB King was also brought in, which was so exciting. Unfortunately, he was having health issues and it was hard for him to travel, so Scott went out to Las Vegas to record his parts in a small studio where BB preferred to work.

King's vocals and guitar work were featured on "Early in the Mornin'," with Allen Toussaint on keyboards.[6]Allen was himself a legend in the New Orleans R&B community, producing "Right Place, Wrong Time" by Dr. John, and "Lady Marmalade" by Labelle, among many other iconic artists. He was also featured on "Shattered Dreams" and "Mother Earth."

Everybody was in awe of guitar player, Charles "Skip" Pitts. In 1970, he moved to Memphis to join Isaac Hayes' band, and is considered one of the greatest R&B guitarists, ever.[7] What everyone remembered him most for was his distinctive "*Wah-Wah*" style of playing, and the extraordinary guitar riff he created for the soundtrack of the 1971 film *Shaft*, which ultimately earned Isaac Hayes an Academy Award.

When Skip arrived at the studio, we all gathered around him like little kids, begging: "Could you please play the 'Shaft' riff?"

He was kind enough to play it, so of course we needed to hear it at least a dozen more times. It left us with an incredibly joyous feeing. Needless to say, he was sensational on the album.

Unfortunately, Skip was not in the best of health, and although he did join Cyndi on the road at some point, it wasn't for long.[8] Some of the other musicians on the album joined her on tour as well, which made for some explosive and exciting performances.

The album, *Memphis Blues*, is a tour de force. It was number one on the Billboard Top Blues chart for thirteen weeks, was nominated for a Grammy, and the tour supporting the album went to every inhabited continent on earth.

> I get full of good liquor, walk the streets all night/Go home and put my man out if he don't act right," sings Cyndi Lauper, sounding perfectly enchanted by the prospect, on this album's last track, "Wild Women Don't Get the Blues." It's a satisfying conclusion to a record that answers a question nobody was actually asking—Can Lauper carry off an LP of blues cover version?—with a definitive "yes."[9]

❅   ❅   ❅

The first stop we made in Memphis, however—before we even started recording—fired up our energy and artistic passion in a profound way.

The day before the recording was to begin, Cyndi and I visited downtown Memphis.

We took the trolley to the National Civil Rights Museum. Neither of us had been on a trolley before, and it was a bit rickety but a lot of fun. We snapped some photos while on the ride and were having a terrific time. As we approached downtown, I suggested we get off a block or two early before we arrived at the infamous Lorraine Motel—to look around.

And who we found—was Jacqueline Smith.

> After twenty-six years and 124 days, Jacqueline Smith is still standing under her blue tarp and umbrella at the corner of Butler and Mulberry Street in Memphis, the location of what used to be the Lorraine Motel. . . . In front of her, two white Cadillacs are parked below the balcony of Room 306, the place where Dr. Martin Luther King took his last breath after he was shot by James Earl Ray, April 4, 1968 at 6:01p.m.[10]

After Dr. King was assassinated, the Lorraine continued operating and Room 306 was left intact. "The bed is made. The food tray is on the coffee table. The ashtray with a partially smoked cigarette is on the desk." [11] It looks exactly the same as it did on that fatal day—frozen in time.

But in 1988, the state of Tennessee decided to make the motel part of the National Civil Rights Museum. The city of Memphis evicted everyone from the Lorraine—which was also an SRO—but Jacqueline Smith, a desk clerk, and resident there since 1968, refused to leave.

> Four sheriff's deputies today evicted the last resident of the Lorraine Motel, where the Rev. Dr. Martin Luther King Jr. was assassinated 20 years ago . . . Randy Wade, an administrative assistant for the Shelby County sheriff's office, said deputies used a tire iron to force open the door to Miss Smith's room. [12]

It was a very emotional experience. When we first got to the Lorraine, we went up the front stairs. There was a big glass window through which we looked—holding our breath—into Room 306. It shook us to the core.

When we went back down the stairs, we crossed the street over to Jacqueline, who was sitting at a desk with protest signs in front of her.

At that point, in 2010, it had been twenty-two years since Jacqueline was sitting in quiet protest, and she was still there.

As we approached her, she suddenly jumped up and started singing "Girls Just Wanna Have Fun." It was so surprising—it made us both smile, which was a little unexpected, given the heavy significance of where we were.

She was very kind and started speaking to us about the civil rights movement, the Civil Rights Museum and the gentrification that was going on everywhere. She felt very strongly that the city had wasted its money on things that could have been put to better use, that resources had not gone to supporting the rights of African Americans living and struggling today. Instead, it capitalizes on the dead—Dr. King and Elvis Presley.

> Memphis, which she sites as the second most segregated city in America, would better serve the teachings of Dr. King if they addressed the problems

of the homeless such as hunger, drug addiction and crime rather than displacing people from the few affordable shelters in the area (in 2002 the museum displaced more people with the acquisition [of] the boarding house across the street where it is believed Ray made the fatal shot).[13]

She remains there to this day, a true hero, continuing to advocate for Dr. Martin Luther King, Jr.'s teachings.

> "The well off and the secure have too often become indifferent and oblivious to the poverty and deprivation in their midst. Ultimately, a great nation is a compassionate nation. . . . No individual or nation can be great if it does not have a concern for 'the least of these.'"[14]

—Dr. Martin Luther King, Jr.

33

NEVER FALL IN LOVE WITH A HOOKER

✻ ✻ ✻

One of my regular hustlers that I met in Times Square was Steve. Last week, I saw Steve—he was looking fantastic. Fresh out of jail. White skin with those fabulous freckles. 200 lb. sex god. We also had the best sex ever. We're both positive. The only problem is, and it's a big one, is he's still on drugs. So after one day of fabulous sex, he vanishes and I probably won't hear from him again for a few months. I hear he got one of his legs amputated.

✻ ✻ ✻

I saw this delicious piece of cake in the back pages of yet another publication featuring escort ads. His name is Corey and I am obsessed with him.

✻ ✻ ✻

I now only dream of hustlers, but the medications I take has lowered my craving for them. It all seems like such an effort. But it hasn't stopped me from eyeing every beauty that passes my way.

✿   ✿   ✿

I hear there's been a lot of new recruits in town. Big muscular things. Could be fun. Could be uncut. Could be just what I've held out for all these months.

✿   ✿   ✿

I'm back from Provincetown. It's 1995, July 4th weekend. I love P-town. I met the sexiest, beefiest dancer named Nigel from Montreal. Total babe. We talk music and of course I invite him to NYC.

✿   ✿   ✿

I finally hooked up with the porn star Donnie Russo. Sexy. Totally full of himself. Both got off. But it was a bit stiff. Pun not intended.

✿   ✿   ✿

I put in a call to Mike. Big sexy Italian who knows how to stir up the libido with his filthy mouth, strip tease actions and always with that prick being rock hard.

✿   ✿   ✿

Just had a wonderful session with KC. Such a big, beautiful, beefy guy. Sexy, passionate and not afraid to show off. Loves to get his ass played with, which, by the way, is absolutely stunning.

✿   ✿   ✿

I'm in the UK and had a worked up appetite, first for food then for a prostitute. I found a new bordello called Image on Earls Court on Nevern Square.

The building had a very old Victorian feel to it, with lots of dark wood paneling. When I got there, I met the madame, who was very gracious, and let me know I could see an array of young men down the hall. He told me to follow him. I got to see the young men through a one-way mirror, lounging, watching TV, and playing cards. The madame said I had my pick of the litter. I chose a bodybuilder named Mark who was just what the doctor ordered. He looked a bit challenged, a bit like a Marine and was so playful in bed—big ass, big nipples, lots of dirty talk and a delicious, sloppy kisser. I came twice and made a date for the following evening.

☼ ☼ ☼

There were many one nights stands. There was always some young man who could use a dollar, that I picked up. They were all shapes and sizes and they all had to have a certain look—big, muscular, sometimes freckled, tattooed, built. Now remember, I was in charge, I was paying and they were going to do exactly what I wanted.[1]

☼ ☼ ☼

In late 1994, when I was in San Francisco, I saw an ad for an escort, prominently displayed in the back pages of a local newspaper. One of the reasons it caught my eye was because it said "265 lb. gorgeous man" and the picture was breathtaking. He was total fuckin' beefcake. I called him and when he arrived, he looked exactly as the ad described.

That man turned out to be pro-bodybuilder Chris Duffy who had just won the NPC Nationals in 1992.

> In 1984 he was an overall winner of the Southern States Bodybuilding Championships, and three years later he won two gold medals during NPC Los Angeles Championships. Winning 1992 NPC Nationals, he became Mr. America. He placed second during USA Championships, the same year.[2]

He was on the cover of every muscle and fitness magazine known to man and around that same time, he was appearing in a few adult, gay porn videos directed by Jack Fritscher, which spotlighted posing and muscle worship.

In the mid-90s Duffy pursued a career in gay pornography. He appeared in few movies under the pseudonym—Bull Stanton—but when journalists found out about this, controversies arose, since Duffy was an award-winning, top bodybuilder, and he embodied masculinity.[3]

Chris appeared in these films, so he could escort and make money through sex. He decided to end his contract with Joe Weider's,[4] IFBB (International Federation of Bodybuilders) because Weider wanted him to do too much, for too little money, and because he felt it wasn't right to be working as a bodybuilder while making adult videos.

Not much later after the escort encounter, we started spending time together and there was a definite chemistry between us. We enjoyed the same music, the same movies and going out on the town together. After I went back to New York, Chris came to visit. I met him in my lobby and was again blown away by how completely fuckin' gorgeous he was.

He ended up staying with me for a while, and I so loved his company. I genuinely liked the idea of this guy in my life because when things got hectic, just the small action of walking down the street, hand in hand, was so romantic it took me away from the stress in my life. We would go to movies, galleries, and restaurants. He was incredibly handsome and being with him felt very warm and loving. I also told him I was HIV positive. It was a little scary telling that to somebody who seemed to feel so strongly towards me, but he was fine with it, because I soon found out that *he* was positive, too.

I called him "Big Daddy," and I think he got a kick out of it. But he said that actually, he thought of himself more as "a young boy, run amok." He was so sweet and I had a lot of feelings for Chris—emotions I hadn't had in years.

However, even within the close relationship we were growing into, I sensed that something wasn't quite right. He was in the process of divorcing his second wife and was shooting up steroids and speed, both of which exacerbated his ADD, with which he had recently been diagnosed. In fact, I once found him in my kitchen, crushing up Ritalin tablets and mixing them into his steroid syringe.

I think I wanted Chris to be someone he wasn't and couldn't be at the time. It felt like at some point it was all going to explode—and it did.

Our relationship was always messy—bouncing between New York, San Francisco, and Ft. Lauderdale, managing both of our needs—it became too much. After I had first met him and hired him for one night, we became a couple. But a year later, we broke up. I was miserable about it. It took over all my thoughts and it brought me back into therapy, because I needed to get over him.

Except I didn't. We continued to see each other on and off over the next five years and then at some point we completely lost touch. In 2015, I saw him at the 19th Street Gym in Chelsea, while I was working out. I heard this huge laugh, a laugh that could only belong to one person. I walked over to him. It looked like he was at the end of a very sweaty workout and when he lifted his head, he saw me. I think we were both a little shocked. When that wore off, we smiled and gave each other a huge hug. It was such a surprise to see him again. After that, I saw him a few more times at the gym.

At some point, and I don't know why, I got a nasty email from him. I can only assume he was using drugs again. Drugs had been a big problem for him throughout his life. When I reconnected with him for this book, I found a loving and charming man, who had been working hard on himself and is training to become a professional golfer. This new connection is so vibrant and important and one I hope to keep.

✳   ✳   ✳

In 2010, I was in Los Angeles and walking down Hollywood Boulevard. I came across a construction site and whenever I see a construction site, I make a bee line for it. There was a hot guy there with a tank top on, and I immediately said:

"Hello, Sailor!"

I let him know I was a photographer from NY. His interest seemed to peak immediately, but he said he was super busy, so I suggested we trade phone numbers.

His name was Todd, and he was completely gorgeous, with beautiful, blue eyes. He had long blond hair and a very "surfer dude" quality about him. I found it kind of odd that he was holding down a construction job and I was even more surprised to see, given his very "wasp-y" appearance, that he was completely tattooed from the neck down. I soon found out he danced in strip joints on both the East and West Coasts. Wow . . . *everybody's* got a story.

We connected immediately. And it quickly progressed to something more.

❁   ❁   ❁

My arrangement with Todd lasted a very long time. I constantly paid for him to come to New York and when he was here, essentially, I was his "sugar daddy." I paid for everything. He had a wicked sense of humor and a big dick. I got my needs met and he got to come to New York. He sometimes came for five to ten days, and while he was here, he often did freelance massage work.

At some point, he started having problems with his family—he had kids and a girlfriend—I remember thinking, "What have I got myself into?"— not just because of the obligations with his family, but because he was becoming more important to me than just a trick.

Whenever he left to go back to Los Angeles, it got lonely again. I had become used to him being here. He was sweet and affectionate and he knew how to whip up tasty meals and cater to me. It was a nearly full and complete home life.

In mid-2013, I went to Vegas and I invited Todd to come along. We went to see the Cirque du Soleil show, "The Beatles LOVE." Then out of the blue, I got a call from the tour manager for Guns N' Roses. He said Axl wanted to make a new record and work with a different group of people— so I said okay, I'll go check out the show.

The concert was at The Joint at The Hard Rock Hotel, where we were staying. But halfway through the show we started getting bored with all the guitar solos from the session musicians whom Axl had hired. We then went back to the bar where everybody was hanging out.

We were talking to a number of music people. I had on a $250 Vivienne Westwood T-shirt and all of a sudden, some guy turns around and spills his entire beer all over me. I was furious! I took a deep breath and went upstairs to my room to change.

When the elevator opened on my floor, I got out, and noticed there was a huge window at the end of the hall. I could see all of downtown Vegas when I stood in front of it. As I faced the window, I got down on my knees, and started praying. I was praying because I was aggravated and feeling anxious. Even though I hadn't had a drink for five years, everyone at the show was drinking. It was tough to be around people who were drunk, babbling in my face with the smell of beer and vodka on their breath. Having had a few years under my belt, I didn't have the urge to drink, but it was unpleasant to be around, and I was grateful to be clean and sober.

A few minutes later, another elevator door opened. A group of drunken, rowdy guys got out and saw me on my knees at the window:

"Hey Buddy, are you okay?" they shouted.

"Yes!" I screamed at them. "Leave me alone! I'm praying!"

"*Whoa*!!!" they said, quickly turning around and jamming back into the elevator. I finished praying, rushed back into my room, showered, changed, and headed back downstairs to the show. The guitar solos were still going on—I thought they would never end; I was delighted when it finally did. We then made our way to the Green Room to meet with Axl and discuss what he was looking to do for his new album.

After about an hour of waiting, there was no word from Axl or the tour manager, so we left.

Despite that mix-up, it was another hot weekend with Todd. Of course, all this was at my expense, which I never cared about because he was such a desirable companion. But instead of flying back with me to New York, he returned to Los Angeles.

Five years in, Todd decided he wanted change in his life, to be more involved with this family. And I realized I was tired of the whole setup. He was always a trick. I paid for every single one of those rendezvous. I was sober then and thinking more reflectively on the decisions I was making in my life—I had spent a lot of money on everything for him, and to what end? It was all very one-sided. I was getting nothing out of the whole arrangement. It was time to move forward and not look back.

34

ROUGH GODS

Around 1980, I started using a Polaroid camera. I loved that it was instant and during the process of developing the image, the chemicals merged in such a way that a unique and vibrant color photograph was realized.

At that time, if I wasn't taking concert photos with my 35mm camera, I was taking Polaroids of men I picked up on the street. But I hadn't achieved a complete artistic vision yet or intuition as a professional photographer.

I used my 35mm camera for music portraits and live concert photos, but my Polaroid 600 was strictly for pictures of bodybuilders, construction workers, one-night stands, men who fit into the aesthetic of what I was interested in. Over the years, I've taken tens of thousands of Polaroid images.

After I left the music business in 2004, I decided it was time to start working professionally. The aim was to exhibit my work in established galleries with the ultimate goal of securing a publishing deal.

But then, in 2008, Polaroid began reducing their production and finally shut down their plant.

> Due to marketplace conditions, Polaroid has discontinued almost all of its instant analog hardware products . . . Polaroid has also made the difficult decision to cease manufacturing of instant film products. . . . [1]

I was livid. I scoured every camera store in New York City for Polaroid 600 film. Retailers had now jacked up the prices of the remaining film from $8.99 per pack to $24.99 per pack. Fuji started making instant film at one point, but I didn't like it. Then a company called The Impossible Project[2] launched and purchased the Polaroid patent. They went on to continue making instant analog cameras and film.

The moment it came out, I tried some of their film, but it sucked. I returned all of the film and fought with them to get my money back. About a year later, an application came out on the iPhone called Hipstamatic. It sounded like it would solve all my instant woes because this new app, despite there being no actual film, provided faux film effect in color, classic black & white, and tin type. I was able to extract the images from the iPhone and was surprised to find that I could make exhibition prints up to 30×30 inches in size, with pristine effect. It was a testament to the revolutionary merging of the history of analog cameras with the new technology of the Apple iPhone.

❊   ❊   ❊

In early 2005, I was wandering through the East Village when I came across a store featuring vintage fashion photography, prints, and books. It was owned by a man named Mike Gallagher. We took an immediate liking to each other. I thought Mike was totally fabulous.

The store was on the corner of East 11st and 4th Avenue, and it was called Gallagher's Paper Collectibles.[3] It sold every fashion magazine in history—*Vogue, Elle, Harper's Bazaar*—some dating back further than 100 years. The main space was on the first floor and the archives were in the basement. Mike was friends with many well-known artists and photographers, such as Bert Stern, known for Marilyn Monroe's "The Last Sitting," as well as Henri Cartier Bresson, Steven Meisel, and Richard Avedon. Mike's basement had the musty smell of aged paper and it was a treasure trove of history.

I told Mike that I took pictures of men and I was looking to get a book deal.

"What kind of pictures again?" he asked, curiously.

"Male erotica."

That surprised him. Mike was heterosexual, and I could sense that he was thinking to himself, "What am I getting myself into?" But Mike liked me and asked me to show him some of my work.

I was delighted and a few days later I came back with about twenty 16 × 20 prints and laid them all out on the floor.

"This is what I do," I said.

"What kind of book do you want to make?" he asked.

"I'm thinking it would combine powerful male portraits with gorgeous flowers to deliver an erotic punch."

He looked at the photographs again.

"You know, let's start small," he said. "I'm going to give you $5,000 dollars for the book you want to make."

I was so grateful. I immediately did research about small printing presses and found one in Canada called Westcan Printing Group. I asked them what I could get accomplished with $5,000.

They were really nice people and told me I could get two thousand copies of the book I wanted to create. So under my own press company—Scatterbrain Press—I printed my first publication and I called it "rough gods." I really liked the way those two words worked together because it reflected 100 percent the type of image I was capturing in my photos. I never photographed professional models because I thought they were much too homogenized. They all looked the same to me. The men I photographed were big, sexy brutes—tattooed, scarred, built.

The book *rough gods* was laid out and designed by my friend Anthony Sellari. It was printed in Canada and a limited selection were numbered and signed. It sold out all two thousand copies.

This slim volume is filled with exactly what you would expect from such a title. The rough-hewn images of masculinity on display here are at once iconic yet accessible. These are no inflatable porn dolls, detached and vaguely unreal in their ascetic roles as visual playthings. These are candid glimpses into the beauty of unvarnished man. Often tattooed, unshaven, and bulging in all of the right places, they never stop being themselves for the camera, creating a surprisingly intimate artistic experience. Often combined with diptych and triptych sets of rusty pipes or stark still life images, these are gods indeed, but the draw is in their unmistakable humanity.[4]

A few months after the book was published, I secured an exhibition at the CBGB Gallery on the Bowery, which was right next door to the original CBGB's club. It was so exciting to have my work finally exhibited for the first time, along with the release of my first book.

At this time, there were other photographers creating images of masculine men but they were more fashion-oriented and extremely glossy. I knew nothing about that approach at all. I think the appeal of my work was that the images were very simple, in a no-nonsense way. They had a raw essence and a quality about them that was very "in-your-face."

The book got into the hands of a publishing company in Berlin called "Bruno Gmünder" and, sometime in 2009, one of their agents called me.

"We would like to make a book with you," he said.

So, I started to figure out the concept for a new book. The words "brutal" and "truth" kept running around in my head. Meanwhile, Sean Lord from s. c. lord design in Baltimore, called me and said he wanted to do an exhibition of my work—even on the telephone, I could tell he was a very kind and caring person, and he understood my "rough gods" concept.

The Baltimore exhibition was so popular I was featured on the cover of the *Gay Life* newspaper, and also in the LGBTQ publication *Baltimore OUTLoud*.

The merging of those words "brutal truth," like the words "rough gods," appealed to me. I liked them because I believed they reflected the artistic vision of the images I was capturing, which were brutal, yet revealed an undeniable truth about the men themselves. I ended up naming the show at s.c. lord design, "Brutal Truth + Beauty."

In this second book, I decided to include poetry along with the photographs of flowers, though it consisted mostly of erotic male portraits. I loved breaking up the rhythm in the book so that each picture would appear more

dramatic. By juxtaposing the images of male erotica with flowers and poetry, when one came upon the photograph of the nude man, it had a much
more profound effect. I also paired certain images, because of a given color
palette, which made them more evocative. Unconsciously, I was inspired by
the ghost of Robert Mapplethorpe. I titled the book, *Brutal Truth*, and it is
a provocative 250-page volume of raw sexuality.

The book sold about five thousand copies. Bruno Gmünder were very
shrewd. I didn't get an advance, but I got two hundred books. I was allowed to sell the book on my own, though not to retailers. I decided to put
word-of-mouth and social media to work and I posted *Brutal Truth* up on
my Rough Gods Facebook page, which had over 100,000 followers. I numbered and signed a small 5 × 7 print and inserted one into each copy of the
book. At first, I made at least $10,000 on my own and then I decided to put
it up on Amazon and sell it at my gallery exhibitions. It was an instant hit
and is now a collector's item.

In between *rough gods* and *Brutal Truth*, I put out a 'zine called *Faggot*,
which focused on a guy named Robert from Canada. He had a tattoo that
read "Faggot" on his stomach, which he proudly displayed. I also started
getting interest from alternative spaces and more prestigious galleries. The
first one was at Brian Marki Fine Arts in Portland, Oregon.

Then I had a show at Magnet, which was in the Castro area of San Francisco. Magnet advertised themselves as: "Men. Sex. Health. Life." It was an
alternative place that offered medical services and psychological services.
They also showed art.

I also had a terrific show in a space in Montreal called "Galerie Den-
taire." It was a dentist's office with a very large front room that looked out
onto Rue Amherst. I had shows in New Orleans, San Diego, New York City
at the LGBT center, and upstate in Hudson, New York, at a furniture store
called F. Collective.

In 2013, I released another book with Gmünder, this one called *Beautiful
Imperfections*. I decided this book would only include photographs I made
with the Hipstamatic app, and there would be no nudity. I wanted this book
to be equally as charged as my previous ones, but I also wanted it to be
more accessible to a wider audience.

I continue to take pictures all the time. For the most part, I have chucked my cameras and mostly shoot with an iPhone, which often surprises the subjects. I may go back to using my digital cameras in the future, but I completely love the Hipstamatic app, and the pristine quality of the images I get from it. The photographs also come out of the camera app in a square frame, which I aesthetically prefer. I get a charge seeing anything in a square. I want everything I shoot to take on a provocative and seductive quality. Whether it's a flower or a heavily tattooed person, I do my best to set a moody and atmospheric tone so that the energy occurring between me and the subject results in an unpredictable and dramatic photograph. As Carol Friedman writes on the inside flap of the book's dust jacket:

> "Sensuality reigns in *Beautiful Imperfections*, where street art, tattooed Romeos, flowers and muscle men are seduced and celebrated by Alago's ever watchful eye."

35

WHO THE FUCK IS THAT GUY?

In 2012, I was backstage at a Cro-Mags gig at the Highline Ballroom in New York City when filmmaker Drew Stone approached me and reintroduced himself. I had not seen Drew in a couple of years since the Misfits European tour. Like myself, Drew is a born and raised New Yorker, who grew up with a passion for music.

Drew had directed a movie that year called *xxx ALL AGES xxx The Boston Hardcore Film*, which was about a small, explosive hardcore music scene in the early eighties. I saw the documentary during its world premiere at the Brattle Theatre in Cambridge, Massachusetts, as part of the Boston International Film festival. I loved that it centered on the community and culture and used a lot of vintage footage revealing unknown facts about the bands featured in the movie.

In a review, the writer stated that "*xxx ALL AGES–The Boston Hardcore Film* feels like a flashback to vibrant memories to anyone that experienced the early Boston scene, and gives a vivid insight . . . that was created in the eighties to all youngsters. It educates on the rise of a highly influential scene that still leaves its marks today."[1]

That night at the Cro-Mags gig, Drew said to me, "I've been thinking about making a new film. Would you like to get together one of these days and have a talk about an idea I have?"

"Sure!" I said, and a few days later, we met at my apartment.

"I think you have an interesting story," he began. "And I believe I'm the right person to tell it. How do you feel about me making a documentary film about your life?"

What?

I didn't know what to say. It sounded really exciting, and of course, my ego got the best of me. Seeing his *Boston Hardcore* film again helped move my thought process along. Since Drew loved music as much as I did, I figured he would do a very good job, and I started to like the whole idea.

Then came the filmmaking process, which was all very new to me. Drew was an independent filmmaker living in the city, and he didn't have the money to finance the film, so we launched a crowdfunding campaign. Many people stepped up and supported the film, including such dear friends as Rob Zombie, Jesse Malin, Gillian McCain, and Cyndi Lauper. Even some of Drew's friends who were involved with his extreme sports films contributed in a big way. We initially raised $30,000, which got us moving in the right direction. Michael Alex was brought in to produce and soon we began to shoot the documentary.

Drew had the idea of introducing some animation into the film in order to move the story along and infuse some humor. That added to budgetary costs, but he thought animating scenes throughout the film was important because it would break it up the rhythm in an entertaining way, as there were a lot of "talking heads" doing interviews and telling stories.

Drew found an animator on Craig's List from Toronto, Canada, named Tim Thomson. He liked Tim's back-to-basics animation work and he sent pictures to him of those of us in the film. Tim sent back drafts of his initial graphics and I had to admit, his illustrations were very close. By the time he sent his second round, he had nailed it. I was totally sold. To this day, I love the animation, and those who have seen it say it's one of the film's highlights.

There were many production delays, the largest of which was scheduling musicians while they were on tour. As a result, filming took nearly four years. Metallica, Rob Zombie, Philip Anselmo, Cyndi Lauper, John Lydon, Mina Caputo, Doyle from the Misfits, and many more were asked to participate. When they agreed I was truly grateful.

Although the working title was "The Michael Alago Documentary," we knew we wanted something more provocative. As we worked more and more on the film, Drew realized that the first thing he remembered about me was when he used to go out to nightclubs during the eighties and nineties—*my* face was the one constant he saw everywhere he went, and he always thought to himself, "Who the fuck *is* that guy?"

When he suggested that as the title, I *knew* that was it. Since the film was a journey through my life, we eventually settled on "Who the Fuck Is That Guy? The Fabulous Journey of Michael Alago."

As the film neared completion, we did a few "work in progress" screenings, one of which drew the attention of filmmaker Peter Spirer. Spirer and Drew had a history of making music videos together back in the eighties, and now his company Rugged Entertainment had a deal with Hollywood distribution company XLrator Media. Spirer absolutely loved the film and a deal was struck for his company to distribute it.

The film debuted on June 8, 2017, at Theater 80 on St. Mark's Place in Manhattan. This was the perfect place for the film to premier because so much of my life took place and was portrayed in that area of the Lower East Side. After a limited theatrical release and a V.O.D. (Video On Demand) run, it was added to Amazon and iTunes. Then, in September, we were ecstatic when it went up on Netflix.

> If the histories of Jimmy Iovine and Dr. Dre warrant four hours of prime HBO real estate in "The Defiant Ones," then certainly Michael Alago, the flamboyant New York punk habitué who signed Metallica to Elektra and White Zombie to Geffen during his stints as an A&R executive, deserves his 77 minutes of recognition. [2]

Netflix was a game changer, because worldwide, *everyone* has Netflix. We were getting messages, texts, and emails from all over the world about the film—social media was exploding. It was an exhilarating feeling. The beauty of it was that viewers came away with a lot of different experiences—from: "Dude, you signed Metallica; that changed the way I listened to music!" to many young people contacting me about their struggle with addiction, recovery and their sexual identity. One message, from a young kid in Colombia, read: "I'm 21 years old, I live in Colombia, I'm HIV-positive. I live with my dad and if I ever told him, I think he would murder me." You can't just reply to an email like that with: "Dude, I'm glad you liked the film." I always wrote back about keeping the faith and taking care of oneself.

I would say to them: "If you're abusing yourself with drugs and alcohol, stop it. If your symptoms are acting up, and it's time to take medications, take them. What's extraordinary about the times we're living in is, if you take care of yourself, and you take your medications, HIV is a treatable disease and you can live a long, healthy life. No matter what the issues are, remember, always ask for help."

That week of September 1, I got twelve hundred emails. So I made an extra cup of tea, sat down, and answered every single one of them.

36

BLANCHE

The living are made of nothing but flaws. The dead, with each passing day in the afterlife, become more and more impeccable to those who remain earthbound.[1]

In January 2017, I found myself in Rutland, Vermont, because my mother had a heart attack. When I got there, she was out of intensive care and in her own room and seemed to be doing well.

Blanche lived independently throughout her senior years until she was ninety-three. At that age, she started to become very forgetful, which manifested in her leaving the front door open, the stove burners on, and the water running in the bathroom. She also suffered a fall, which traumatized her a bit.

Cheryl had been taking care of Mom for the last twenty years. They were very close and spent every day together. They had a humorous, loving, but antagonistic relationship. Mom could be very stubborn. However, after these forgetful incidents, Cheryl had to make the difficult decision to put her in an assisted living facility, where she could be watched over all the time. Since Cheryl was at work during the week, it worried her to leave Mom unattended. She found a place which she thought would work: a Catholic home called The Loretto.

Mom hated every waking moment of it.

Still, she had a lovely little room with three windows and a refrigerator, a telephone, and a huge closet for her clothes and jewelry. All her life, Mom was impeccably dressed—always carefully color-coordinated and exquisitely presented. It aggravated her to no end when she couldn't get everything absolutely right before she left the house—such as having the perfect earrings to match her outfit. She loved yellows and greens in her clothes and one particular red sweater from Loehmann's, which I had given her for Christmas. She spent her days either doing her puzzle, "Word Hunt" or watching B&W movies on TCM. Her favorite shows were *Perry Mason* and *Ironside*, both starring Raymond Burr. When I told her that Raymond Burr was gay, she looked at me incredulously and said: "Not *my* Raymond Burr!" We had a great laugh. Although her mind had started to go, her wit was as sharp as ever and her comic timing was spot-on.

Whenever I visited Mom, I would always bring her plants and gorgeous bouquets of flowers for her windows. One day when I was visiting, she started insisting that she wanted to go back home to Brooklyn, even though she hadn't lived there for twenty years. She also claimed that people at the Loretto were stealing from her.

"Ma," I said, "no one is stealing from you!"

"You don't know, Michael Anthony! "*You* don't live here. They steal from me!" She also started suffering from "Sundowning":

The term "sundowning" refers to a state of confusion occurring in the late afternoon and spanning into the night . . . Sundowning isn't a disease, but a group of symptoms that occur at a specific time of the day that may affect people with dementia, such as Alzheimer's disease. The exact cause of this behavior is unknown. [2]

She would become very difficult to talk to as the day went on. So, I would quickly change the subject, such as:

"Ma! Do you want some French fries from McDonalds?"

Or:

"Would you like to take a walk outside and sit in the rocking chairs together?"

I said whatever I could so her focus wouldn't veer too far into a dark place.

I would also sit close to her and join her in doing her word-search puzzles but once I started taking pictures and shooting video clips of her, she would get annoyed: "I'm making a little movie on you, Ma!" I'd say.

"Don't bother! Leave me alone! I don't take no pictures. I have enough pictures!"

"But this is a little movie, Ma!" I said.

"Oh, shut up!"

"Come *on*, Ma!"

"Oh, all right!"

"I love you!"

"And I adore you!" she said.

I'm so grateful that I knew to make these little clips of Blanche because otherwise I would forget the sound of her voice, which was very important to me. I watch these clips all the time and they fill me with such joy and sometimes even a good cry. Ever since she passed, I have shared the clips on social media. People have loved her salty comments, which were both loving and funny. Blanche was the real deal.

✳   ✳   ✳

After she had the heart attack, she got a little better and was home for a bit. But then she contracted pneumonia. Toward the end of January, she was not feeling well, so Cheryl took her to the hospital.

Cheryl called me, and I immediately packed my bag and got on the five-hour Amtrak train ride to Castleton, Vermont, the last stop in the state. When I arrived, Cheryl's friends, Carol and Linda, picked me up at the station and took me directly to the hospital.

When I walked in and saw her, Mom definitely didn't look good. I said, "Mom, where are your teeth?"

"They stole my teeth!" she insisted.

"Mom, no one stole your teeth! I think you put them in a tissue and acci-dentally threw them away." Well, Mom was one to argue and she continued on with me about the teeth.

"Ma, I'm not here to argue. Let's just relax."

Her breathing was very labored from the pneumonia. It didn't seem like it was getting any better. They gave her some sedatives so she wouldn't be so worried and anxious about it all.

They did all kinds of scans and X-rays, but she really was going downhill. The pneumonia was taking over. She just laid there, barely able to breathe. It was horrible to watch. Our emotions were running high. Fortunately, Linda was a nurse at the same hospital. She and her partner, Carol, were exceptional friends by being there for us as we went through the last hours of my mother's life.

The doctor suggested a very small dose of morphine. Cheryl and I looked at each other, knowing that a little bit of morphine was the beginning of the end. At ninety-four, it was just too difficult to overcome what was happen-ing to her.

During the next three days, we slept at the hospital. On February 2, after the doctor administered some more morphine, Cheryl and I stood close to her hospital bed. I brushed my hand across her forehead and kissed her cheek. It was emotional and very surreal. For a moment, Cheryl walked away; I think it was much too much for her to handle. Then Mom quietly whispered something to me in Spanish, which I didn't understand, so I mentioned it to Cheryl when she returned.

"Michael! She's on morphine, she didn't say anything!"

Cheryl walked back to the side of the bed where I was, and Mom said she loved us and then said, "You two are very funny people."

Those were her last words, and it was very typical of Blanche to inject humor into what was a truly heartbreaking moment.

As Mom was slipping in and out of consciousness, her breathing became more labored and then it stopped. It was near 6 p.m. Cheryl and I started sobbing, in a complete state of shock—not believing she was gone. We continued to kiss her head, her cheek, rub her hands. We didn't want to let go.

Eventually, we were knocked back into reality and we slowly started gathering up her things—a battery-powered, St. Jude light she had gotten at the Dollar Store, her eyeglasses, and the remainder of her clothes.

That night, Cheryl and I went back to Mom's apartment and it all felt so bizarre. We finally needed to get some food, so we went to a local Chinese restaurant and ate, cried, and talked about Mom.

During the last ten years, since I got sober, I had made a commitment to get closer to my mom, to make up for the long period of time I had neglected my family in favor of my career. I then started taking the Amtrak up to Castleton to see her every six weeks.

It was a blessing to be able to get to know her again over those long weekends. Sometimes those visits with her were very quiet but they were so important and made all the difference in the world to me. They were often about the little things like holding hands and watching black-and-white movies together. We always had a good laugh which made those visits even more poignant.

I also called her every morning after my AA meeting. When she died, and I realized I would no longer have those routines with my mom—that was the beginning of a very different world for me.

Keep yourselves in God's love as you wait for the mercy of our Lord Jesus Christ to bring you to eternal life.

—St. Jude

37

GRATITUDE

God grant me the serenity
to accept the things I cannot change,
Courage to change the things I can,
And the wisdom to know the difference.[1]

On October 21, 2007, I started attending a twelve-step program and I have never stopped.

For years, everyone had seen me totally plastered, night after night, crawling from club to club, from party to party. Many nights, when I got to a point where I was barely conscious, my friends threw me into a cab and sent me home, praying I'd get there safely. Little did they know, I often ended up in a knock-down, drag-out fight with the cab driver because he wouldn't let me smoke crack in the back of his taxi. Believe it or not, I thought this was normal behavior.

But that day, in October, 2007, I knew it was time to change my life. I was sick and tired of my behavior—I had to get some serious help.

Those first few twelve-step meetings were a complete blur. It was frightening, because I was hoping that I could actually get sober and, of course, the trick of it all is to stay sober one day at a time. I was run down and depleted. I felt like a zombie and my immune system totally sucked. Once again, it was being completely compromised. I had been taking my HIV meds with alcohol and drugs for so long, I could feel my body completely falling apart. I thought to myself: I *How could I continue to take my meds this way?* I was totally overwhelmed. I worried I might lose my strength to go forward.

But something kept me moving. When I arrived at the front door of the meeting place, I had serious hesitation about going in. My mind and my body were filled with fear and shame. I was mortified. I had ruined so much in my life, had been so irresponsible to the people I loved, and now I found myself taking the biggest step ever by walking through that door.

In the early days of attending meetings, it is suggested that you raise your hand as early as possible and say your first name followed by "I'm an alcoholic." That's what I did, and I felt a small sense of relief, like I could start breathing again.

It was also suggested that I get a sponsor. I asked a dear friend I had known for years who had double-digit sobriety if he might fill that important role; he said he would. His first suggestion was for me to go to ninety meetings in ninety days. That process gives you a sober routine so that by the end of the ninety-day period you could feel the toxins leaving your body, rerouting your brain chemistry to the point where you begin to feel a glimmer of hope.

On the ninetieth day, I decided to share my story. In the middle of the room, up against the wall, there is a small table and chair where the guest speaker sits to "qualify."[2] But the moment I sat down to tell my story, I put my head on the desk and just sobbed uncontrollably. I don't remember how long it took me to pull myself together, but when I did, I told everyone about my messed-up, fucked-up, drugged-up, alcoholic life. I had been a complete no-show for every single event my family and friends had invited me to, never mind that I was a liar and a thief as well. I talked about how my friends and family couldn't count on me for anything. I spoke about how I didn't pay attention to many important things in my life for so many years.

I couldn't believe I was sitting in that chair telling the whole awful truth about myself to a roomful of strangers—the complete, unvarnished truth. Really, for the first time, I was being totally honest with myself. I started to feel enormous freedom. I felt my body relaxing. It was the beginning of a huge turning point in my life.

I've met some fascinating people at the meetings. We may all come from different walks of life, but we end up in the same place. At the heart of it all, we're just a group of drunks looking to get sober one day at a time. That collective energy—of wanting to get sober—empowers each of us as we, "made a decision to turn our will and our lives over to the care of God as we understand Him."[3]

I've learned many lessons in my sober life. Because of my renewed faith in God, whenever I wake up with fear, manifesting itself as anxiety, and my mind starts telling me that I'm not good enough, wondering if anyone will ever love me, that I'm fifty-nine years old and may never get a job again—I know those thoughts were part of an old tape in an old life that played in my head endlessly. I have learned so much in my twelve-step program, so when my mind becomes filled with those old worries, it now quickly changes and is replaced with prayer. My belief in God moves me to live in faith, hope, and love so that I have peace of mind at the end of each and every day.

My life in sobriety is very rich and full and I feel like I can do anything. I am now becoming the person I have always wanted to be. Friends and family know that I'm reliable and responsible and they can count on me. I am here to be of good service to everyone that I meet.

Life is still such a mystery to me, though I have learned many valuable lessons along the way. And the most important lesson I have learned is to live in love and not fear. It took me a long time to get there. I know many strive for perfection, which I don't believe exists. But what I do know is that I work on myself every day to be the best person I can be, so that I can show compassion and gratitude to everyone I encounter.

It's been twelve years now and I still go to meetings every day, Monday through Friday. When I wake up in the morning, I make my bed, I boil water for tea, and then I get on my knees to pray. All of the prayers are filled with gratitude.

Thank you, God, for waking me up.

Thank you for waking me up sober.

Thank you for my twelve-step program.

Thank you for my sponsor.

Thank you for my mom.

Thank you for my renewed relationship with my sister, Cheryl.

Since there are usually so many people to thank, that gratitude list sometimes goes on forever, yet it fills me with such joy. I usually add the prayers I had grown up saying in the Catholic Church: the Our Father, the Hail Mary, and the Glory Be. When I finish, I put on my hat, coat, and shoes, and go out the door to take on the world, and I always say the Serenity Prayer as I leave.

I also find inspiration from authors and thinkers such as: Charles Bukowski, John O'Donohue, Hilda Charlton, Sister Joan Chittister, Rumi, Mary Oliver, Patti Smith, and James Baldwin.

In the end, the beauty of being sober is that I show up for life. I showed up for my mom's life. I continue to show up for Cheryl's life. I show up for my own life. How wonderful it is to be present and grateful, to acknowledge all the gifts we are given each and every day . . . as this amazing journey continues.

ACKNOWLEDGMENTS

Hi Mom, I love you and I miss you every single day. You live in my heart and continue to watch over me, so I know everything will always be A-OK.

Dad, you left us way too early and I wish we could have had a closer relationship. All my love. RIP.

Cheryl Ann Alago—you are the best sister ever and I love our relationship. You mean the world to me.

Vince Aletti—Your brilliance always inspires me. Let's continue exchanging naughty photos!

Philip Anselmo—Hi PA . . . you beast! I love everything about you. You are an amazing soul. Love, MA

Jerry Brandt—Thank you for being a wonderful mentor and friend. I learned so much from you. Much love.

Dennis Bremser—Hello there, superstar in heaven. You will forever hold a special place in my heart. I love you and miss our conversations. God bless you.

Phil Caivano—My Rock 'n' Roll brother from another mother. Marry me already! Love you, my friend. God bless you.

Mina Caputo—You are love, light, and the truth. Love you forever.

John Cerullo—Thank you for your expertise in helping to put together this book.

Loren Chodosh—You are kind and loving and certainly know how to take care of business. I am grateful to have you in my life.

Peter Crowley—We go way back! Thank you for getting my first photographs published. I have always been very fond of you.

Doyle—You great big, beautiful man. You are my angel!

Chris Duffy—You big hunka love. You entered my life in the most unusual and fun-loving way. Thank you for being there.

George Dureau—I am filled with so much love for our thirty-year friendship. You were one of a kind. RIP.

Tim Ebneth—Our longtime friendship means the world to me. We have been through so much together. I love you.

Bob Feiden—You would be so proud of me. RIP.

Danny Fields—Thank you so much for a lifetime of love and laughter and all the gorgeous Polaroids of the tricks and the trade.

Carol Friedman—You are brilliant and gorgeous. I cherish our longtime friendship. You have been by my side through it all. I love you!

Keith Guldalian—Thank you for being in my life at the right time.

Ian Jopson—Darling Ian, I am grateful for our friendship from the day we met. I am sure it will last a lifetime. Much love.

John Joseph—Stay healthy, stay brilliant . . . I love you!

Bob Krasnow—You were a genius. Thank you for taking me under your wing as well as over to Madison Avenue for a great shoe shine! You were definitely a unique human being and I feel honored to have known you. RIP.

Mitchell Krasnow—Thank you for telling Bob about me. You helped change the course of my life. You will always be very special to me.

Liz Lamere and Dante Vega Lamere—Love you both! Your husband and dad, Alan Vega, lives in our hearts and still inspires us in all that we do.

Cyndi Lauper—Love you! Memphis was quite the experience. I hope to work with you again.

John Lydon—What can I say? You are a true original. I cherish our thirty-eight years of friendship, looking forward to many more.

Diana Mahiques—You are truth and beauty and your spiritual energy is infectious. Thank you.

Robert Mapplethorpe—I loved knowing you. Your exquisite photographs continue to inspire and stimulate me. RIP.

Jimmy Marino—Everybody loves you but not more than me.

Gillian McCain—You have a wonderful heart and radiate true generosity of spirit. Thank you for always showing up for me and being a great friend.

Dito Montiel—I completely adore you. We will forever be in each other's lives.

Toni Quirk—Your charm, wit, and intelligence bring out the best in every-one who meets you. You were a treasure for me when we worked together, and you are a beautiful individual.

Brian Regnaert—I have always been grateful that you came in to my life. You are an angel and I love you.

Daniel Rey—Wow! Almost forty years of friendship. Thank you, my friend and dear confidant.

Kane Roberts—You are totally fabuleen! You have the biggest rock n' roll heart of anybody that I know. You ain't gettin' rid of me anytime soon!

Ira Silverberg—Our friendship has covered the waterfront—books, gossip, and rock n roll—you're brilliant, you're crazy. I love you.

Nina Simone—I love you and miss you. We had the best times together. RIP.

Patti Smith—You have been an inspiration to me my entire life. Thank you for all the telephone calls through my darkest hours. The wit and wisdom of those calls kept me alive.

Lee Sobel—Thank you for encouraging me to write this book.

Debbie Southwood-Smith—We have had so many years together. Through all the ups and downs, we are still here! Much love!

Barbara Starrett, MD—Always love and respect. Thank you for literally saving my life.

Drew Stone—Thank you, my friend, for making a documentary about my life—it created the interest in getting this book made.

Arturo Vega—Your friendship will always live in my heart. RIP, brother.

Sean Yseult—You are completely fabulous and an awesome friend. I am blessed to have you in my life!

Love and Gratitude:

Eric AK, Matthew Alago, Gloria Alago, Michael Alex, Carole Ann Avramides, Bill Avramides, Sunny Bak, Joseph Baldassare, Lisa Barbaris, Stiv Bators, Barbara Bermudez, Chris Blackwell, Johnny Blitz, Eric Bogosian, Scott Bomar, Mike Bone, Steven Ames Brown, Bill Brusca; Cliff Burton, Nick Calderazzo, Tim Cameron, Clare Cerullo, Melissa Corrales Campagna, Lionel Casseroux, Frank Caston, Cheetah Chrome, Barbara Claire, Joshua Coburn, Aida Colon, Marlon Connolly, Demetrius Constantinus, Jayne County, Ether Coven, Patrick Dalton, Tim Dax, James DeMaria, Joseph D'Emic, Ivan de Prume, Antone DeSantis, Donna Destri, Sandy Dillon, Sherman Ewing, Tom Eubanks, Diane Farris, Gigi Faz, Andre Fischer, Michael Fisher, Roxanne Fontana, Foxy, Jack Fritscher, Mike Gallagher, James Gavin, Michael Gilbert, Michael Gira, Alex Gildzen, David Godlis, Luis Gonzalez, Marty Grabill, Lisa Greco, Jonathan Greenfield, Thaddeus Jones, Kirk Hammett, Harden Harrison, Harry, Hazelden, Diane Hensley, James Hetfield, Jeff Hirshberg, Hilary Hodgson, Gary Holt, Emily Hughes, Chris Jericho, Constance Jones, David Kahauolopua, Jessica Kastner, Joe Katz, Al Kavadlo, Danny Kavadlo, Lenny Kaye, Pat Kepic, Laura Keyes, Jacque Kochevar, Hilly Krystal, Helena Van Leirsberghe, Scott Lucas, George Lynch, Ray Majors, Bernadette Malavarca, Manny the Greek from Astoria, Jeff Marshall, Linda McKenna, Carol McKenna, Rod McKuen, Frank Micari, Charlie Mills, Bob Morris, Richard Munguia, Nina Murano, Katie Nachod, Mary Navarro, Jason Newsted, Nicole Newsted, Jerry Only, Danny Papa, Maria Papa, Corrin Papa-Alicea, Jennifer Papa-Micari, Louise Parnassa Staley, Kevin Patrick, Jessica Pimentel, Jack Ponti, Genesis P-Orridge, Ursula Quiñones, Jennie Ramos, John Ramos, Lori Reese, Bubba Richards, Kate Richardson, Jody Robello-Katz, Jamie Robinson, Izzy Rodriguez, Julie Rodriguez, Arthur Roger, Joe Russo, Saint Jude, Saint Therese of the Roses, Patrick Sarfati, Beth Schiffer, Michael Schmidt, Eric Alan Schmidt, Anthony Sellari, Bernie Shanahan, Gary Simmons, Lisa Simone, Kris Sims, Rodney Skleton, Kelly Smith, Ronnie Spector, Linda Stein,

Stanley Stellar, Rambo Stevens, Leslie Swiman, Joe Sztabnik, Sandra Torres, Sylvia Torres, Suki-Marie Treiber, Mat Treiber, Arthur Tress, Susan Henderson Tyler, Lars Ulrich, Kurdt Vanderhoof, Cherry Vanilla, Rich Varecha, Tom Viola, Diane Vocaturo, Rich Ward, Keith Webb, Rob Youells, Jay Yuenger, Jon and Marsha Zazula, Jimmy Zero, Rob Zombie, Paul Zone

If my scatterbrain forgot anyone, I promise that the next time I see you— you will be in for a great big hug and a smooch!

Laura—Thank you for all the hard work you put in helping to tell my story. Despite all the kerfuffle . . . I could not have done it without you. Love, Michael

With Laura. (© GODLIS)

NOTES

INTRODUCTION

1. John O'Donohue, *Anam Cara: A Book of Celtic Wisdom* (New York: Harper Perennial, 2004), p. 18.

2. https://pleasekillme.com/gay-metal/

3. https://variety.com/2017/film/news/michael-alago-who-signed-metallica -and-white-zombie-gets-the-documentary-treatment-in-who-the-fk-is-that -guy-1202497423/

CHAPTER 2. VULNERABLE

1. Saunders, Mike (May 1971). "*Kingdom Come* review". *Creem*. Archived from the original on 2007-03-08. Retrieved 2007-02-14.

CHAPTER 4. PATTI

1. Patti Smith, *Early Work 1970-1979*, 2nd edition (New York: W. W. Norton & Company, 1995); "To the Reader", p. x.

2. Liner notes, *Horses*, Arista Records (1975).

3. Phone call with Patti Smith, March 1994.

4. Pier Paolo Pasolini, *Roman Poems* (San Francisco: City Lights Books, 2001).

5. Patti Smith, *The Coral Sea*, Revised Edition (New York: W.W. Norton, 2012), "The Final Flower," p. 23.

CHAPTER 5. A NEW FAMILY

1. http://thequietus.com/articles/20590-alan-vega-obit-obituary-suicide

2. https://www.vulture.com/2016/07/alan-vega-suicide-frontman-dead-at-78.html

CHAPTER 7. 10½ INCHES

1. https://www.therialtoreport.com/2017/02/19/marc-stevens/

CHAPTER 8. FLORIDA. BOSTON. NEW YORK.

1. https://www.bbc.co.uk/bbcthree/article/3e75b380-f622-4345-a383-4f948fc1013c

2. http://archive.boston.com/ae/theater_arts/articles/2010/03/07/taking_a_sidewalk_stroll_on_the_seedy_side_of_the_combat_zone/

CHAPTER 9. ALL THIS AND MORE

1. https://www.nytimes.com/2013/06/12/arts/music/arturo-vega-spokesman-and-designer-for-the-ramones-dies-at-65.html

CHAPTER 10. MULTIPLE EXPOSURE

1. By Michael Alago, 1979. Author's collection.

CHAPTER 11. THE RITZ

1. Tim Sommer, Press Review, *Sounds*, May 30, 1981. http://www.fodderstompf.com/GIG%20LIST/rit81.html

2. https://www.youtube.com/watch?v=6Ru6TuywY-0&feature=youtube

3. Tim Sommer, Press Review, *Sounds*, May 30, 1981. http://www.fodderstompf.com/GIG%20LIST/rit81.html

4. https://www.nytimes.com/2010/05/20/arts/music/20pil.html

CHAPTER 12. WAR ZONE

1. https://www.nytimes.com/1982/07/18/nyregion/city-seeks-to-dislodge-drug-trade-by-demolishing-tenement-havens.html

2. https://www.nytimes.com/2014/12/28/nyregion/iggy-lou-joey-and-danny.html

CHAPTER 13. RED PARROT

1. John Sex was a cabaret singer and performance artist until he died in 1990, at the age of thirty-four from AIDS complications.

2. http://articles.latimes.com/1988-10-12/news/mn-3319_1_wayland-flowers

3. http://observer.com/2017/02/capitalism-has-suppressed-black-musicians/

CHAPTER 15. AMERICAN DREAMER

1. https://www.nytimes.com/2004/10/17/arts/music/just-what-they-needed.html

2. Mary Dearborn, *Mailer: A Biography*, Reprint edition (New York: Mariner Books, 2001), p. 353.

CHAPTER 17. METALLICA

1. Island Records president (1990–1991), Mercury co-president (1991), Def American Minster of Truth (1992–1994).

CHAPTER 18. FORCE TO BE RECKONED WITH

1. From the documentary, *Who the Fuck Is That Guy?: The Fabulous Journey of Michael Alago*, directed by Drew Stone, produced by Michael Alex.

2. https://www.rollingstone.com/music/music-lists/the-100-greatest-metal-albums-of-all-time-113614/metallica-master-of-puppets-1986-3-194128/

3. The bus driver was cleared of any wrongdoing.

4. http://ultimateclassicrock.com/metallica-bassist-cliff-burton-dies-in-a-bus-accident/

CHAPTER 19. THAT METAL GUY

1. https://loudwire.com/best-thrash-albums-not-released-by-big-4/

2. https://www.apnews.com/7214ac27d974afc9c5c0aa08cf633643

CHAPTER 20. HIV ANONYMOUS

1. https://www.avert.org/professionals/history-hiv-aids/overview#footnote6_4xcwand

2. http://www.anothermag.com/art-photography/3370/under-the-piers-alvin-baltrops-gay-new-york

3. "Known for her selfless devotion to her patients, Dr. Starrett is loved by many New Yorkers. She has been acknowledged for her work with the Health Services Award of the Gay and Lesbian Independent Democrats, the Michael Hirsch Award from Body Positive, the Emery Hetrick Award from the Hetrick-Martin Institute, and she was recognized at World AIDS Day 2005 by New York City Mayor Michael Bloomberg." http://amfar.org/in-the-spotlight/awards-of-courage/2007-honoring-with-pride-barbara-starrett,-m-d-/

4. http://science.sciencemag.org/content/224/4648/475; https://www.theaidsinstitute.org/education/aids-101/where-did-hiv-come-0

5. https://cvi.asm.org/content/23/4/249

With Nina Simone, 1993. (© Carol Friedman)

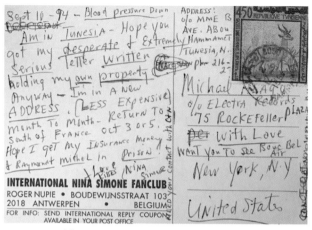

Postcard from Nina Simone, 1994. (Author Collection)

*Nina Simone A Single Woman
album cover, 1993. (© Carol Friedman)*

*With Nina late night at her apartment in West
Hollywood, CA, 1992. (Author Collection)*

*Polaroid collage of Foxy, the meanest 22 yr.-old cat in NY, and my sweet
and adorable Brian Regnaert, 1994. (© Michael Alago)*

Frank with kittens at Louisiana State Prison, 2017.(Author Collection)

Marty at Airway Heights Corrections Center, Washington State, 2004. (Author Collection)

With Jerry Only of the Misfits, 2016. (Author Collection)

All Access American Psycho Tour laminate, 1997. (Author Collection)

Obey Misfits graffiti, Wynwood, Miami, Florida, 2016. (© Michael Alago)

Portrait of Hilly Kristal, New York City, 2006. (© Michael Alago)

After Hurricane Katrina, Fats Domino's home, Lower 9th Ward, New Orleans, 2007. (Author Collection)

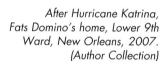

Michael Alago, Studio Portrait, 1993. (© Stanley Stellar)

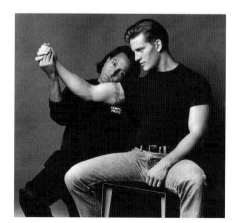

Michael and Brian, 1993. (© Stanley Stellar)

2018 selfie with Mina Caputo and Carol Friedman. (© Carol Friedman)

With Carol Friedman, 2019. (© Carol Friedman)

Visiting Robert Mapplethorpe's grave with Patti Smith, Lenny Kaye, and Edward Mapplethorpe on the 20th anniversary of his death, March, 2009. (Author Collection)

In front of the Lorraine Motel, Memphis, Tennessee, 2010. (Author Collection)

Cyndi Lauper and Jacqueline Smith outside the Lorraine Motel, Memphis, Tennessee, 2010. (Author Collection)

With Jacqueline Smith outside the Lorraine Motel, Memphis, Tennessee, 2010. (Author Collection)

Historic sign showing how long Jacqueline Smith has been standing in protest outside the Lorraine Motel, Memphis, Tennessee, 2010. (Author Collection)

With Cyndi Lauper, on the set of "Who the F**k is that Guy?," New York City, 2014. (Photo by helenabxl)

Current portraits shot with The Hipstamatic App., 2017–18. Top Left to Right: Al Kavadlo, Kris Sims, Left to Right Bottom: Thaddeus Jones, Danny Kavadlo. (© Michael Alago)

My mom, Blanche, with her beloved St. Jude Statue, 2016. (Author Collection)

Alago Family Portrait: Cheryl, Mom, and me, 2016. (Author Collection)

CHAPTER 21. FAT AND FELT

1. http://shin-gallery.com/Artist/ArtistsView.aspx?ArtistCd=45

2. https://www.theguardian.com/artanddesign/2016/jan/30/fat-felt-fall-earth-making-and-myths-joseph-beuys

3. https://tayandhergay.blogspot.com/2012/11/plight-by-joseph-beuys-1985.html

4. Joseph Beuys, Propyläen; 1. Aufl edition (1975).

5. Joseph Beuys,Verlag Ullstein GmBH, Frankfurt-am-Main-Berlin-Wein, Propyläen Verlag (1975).

6. Joseph Beuys, PrestelVerlag, München (1981).

7. Beuys also appeared in productions with Douglas Davis—father of co-writer, Laura—most famously in *Documenta 6* in Kassel, Germany, along with Nam Jun Paik. https://www.eai.org/titles/a-conversation.

8. http://www.artnet.com/artists/joseph-beuys/

CHAPTER 22. HUMANITY

1. Philip Geftner, "George Dureau: The Photographs," *Aperture*, May 24, 2016, p. 11.

2. https://www.dazeddigital.com/photography/article/32507/1/george-dureau-the-artist-said-to-have-influenced-mapplethorpe-the-most

3. https://www.nytimes.com/2012/06/22/arts/design/george-dureau-black-1973-1986.html

4. http://arthurrogergallery.com/2014/04/george-dureau-new-orleans-master-painter-photographer-died-times-picayune/

5. Philip Gefter, *George Dureau, The Photographs* (New York: Aperture, 2016), First Edition.

6. https://obits.nola.com/obituaries/nola/obituary.aspx?n=george-valentine-dureau&pid=170659712&fhid=5630

CHAPTER 23. THE PERFECT MOMENT

1. https://www.nytimes.com/2012/06/22/arts/design/george-dureau-black-1973-1986.html

2. https://www.pictadesk.com/post/BWCjBiwl-Kq

CHAPTER 24. ROLLING THE DICE

1. Rosemary *Passatino,* "Swans: Burning World" *Spin, August 1989, p. 82.*

2. Deele Fadele, Nick Soulsby, *Swans: Sacrifice And Transcendence: The Oral History* (Minneapolis, MN: JAWBONE Press, 2018), p. 154.

3. https://www.history.com/this-day-in-history/three-members-of-the-southern -rock-band-lynyrd-skynyrd-die-in-a-mississippi-plane-crashie

CHAPTER 25. HAZELDEN

1. Author's Collection.

2. Ibid.

CHAPTER 26. A SINGLE WOMAN

1. https://www.out.com/entertainment/popnography/2012/04/04/catching -rough-gods-michael-alago

2. https://www.nytimes.com/1983/06/06/arts/cabaret-nina-simone.html

3. https://www.thevintagenews.com/2017/02/08/at-her-first-recital-12-year -old-nina-simone-refused-to-start-singing-after-her-parents-were-moved-from-the -front-row-to-make-room-for-whites/

4. https://www.biography.com/people/nina-simone-9484532

5. "A Single Woman" liner notes by Ntozake Shange.

6. https://www.rollingstone.com/music/music-album-reviews/a-single -woman-252835/

7. http://jamesgavin.com/page6/page58/page58.html

8. Letter from Nina Simone, 1993. Author's collection.

9. Phone call with Nina, February 22, 1995. Author's collection.

10. https://www.theguardian.com/music/1999/jul/03/meltdownfestival1999 .meltdownfestival

11. http://boscarol.com/ninasimone/pages/nina/concerts/1999-Royal.html

12. *Ibid.*

CHAPTER 27. I DREAMED I DRANK A NIGHTMARE

1. Tom Eubanks, *Ghosts of St. Vincent's* (New York: BookBaby, 2017), Kindle Edition, p. 77.

2. https://www.hiv.gov/hiv-basics/overview/history/hiv-and-AIDS-timeline

3. Eubanks, *Ghosts of St. Vincent's*, p. 96.

4. *Ibid.*, p. 97.

5. PCP (or pneumocystis pneumonia) is the most common opportunistic infection in people with HIV. Without treatment, over 85% of people with HIV would eventually develop PCP. It has been the major killer of people with HIV. However, PCP is now almost entirely preventable and treatable. (http://www.AIDSinfonet .org/fact_sheets/view/537)

6. https://aidsinfo.nih.gov/drugs/25/pentamidine/0/professional

7. Eubanks, *Ghosts of St. Vincent's*, p. 147.

8. https://www.seattletimes.com/seattle-news/at-height-of-AIDS-crisis-nurse -ran-secret-leftover-drug-pipeline/

9. Toxoplasmosis is considered to be a leading cause of death attributed to foodborne illness in the United States. More than 30 million men, women, and children in the U.S. carry the *Toxoplasma* parasite, but very few have symptoms because the immune system usually keeps the parasite from causing illness. (https:// www.cdc.gov/parasites/toxoplasmosis/index.html)

10. Excerpt from personal journal.

11. "Observation Poem" by Michael Alago.

12. Zidovudine is used to treat HIV, the virus that can cause acquired immuno-deficiency syndrome (AIDS). Zidovudine is also given during pregnancy to prevent an HIV-infected woman from passing the virus to her baby. Zidovudine is not a cure for HIV or AIDS. (https://www.drugs.com/mtm/zidovudine.html)

13. http://time.com/4705809/first-AIDS-drug-azt/

14. *Ibid.*

15. https://www.independent.co.uk/arts-entertainment/the-rise-and-fall -of-azt-it-was-the-drug-that-had-to-work-it-brought-hope-to-people-with-hiv -and-2320491.html

16. https://www.fda.gov/forpatients/illness/hivAIDS/history/ucm151079.htm#95

17. https://www.healthline.com/health/hiv-aids/understanding-the-aids-cocktail

18. https://www.cdc.gov/mmwr/preview/mmwrhtml/mm6021a2.htm.

19. https://www.avert.org/professionals/history-hiv-AIDS/origin#footnote5_dw fqgbf

20. Eubanks, *Ghosts of St. Vincent's*, p. 179.

CHAPTER 28. AMERICAN PSYCHO

1. http://articles.latimes.com/1994-07-13/business/fi-15128_1_warner-music

CHAPTER 29. PRISON MATES

1. https://www.imdb.com/title/tt0112818/

2. Prejean, Helen (1993). Dead Man Walking. Random House. ISBN 0-679-75131-9

3. https://www.sisterhelen.org/biography/

CHAPTER 30. NO MORE MR. RECORD EXECUTIVE

1. https://www.allmusic.com/artist/mike-shipley-mn0000485325/biography

2. http://www.ew.com/article/2002/03/08/here-comes-zoo/

3. http://gothamist.com/2016/07/18/jack_douglas_john_lennon_interview.php

4. https://www.quora.com/What-did-it-smell-like-on-9-11-after-the-collapse

5. The photograph appears as the last shot of *Burning Down the House: The Story of CBGB's*, directed by Mandy Stein. (2009).

6. https://www.nytimes.com/2007/08/30/arts/music/30kristal.html

7. https://www.livescience.com/22522-hurricane-katrina-facts.html

8. https://www.washingtonpost.com/news/the-fix/wp/2015/08/29/the-hurricane-katrina-x-codes-art-politics-controversy-and-now-reform/?noredirect=on&utm_term=.691424651a12

9. https://www.independent.co.uk/arts-entertainment/music/news/fats-domino-katrina-dead-hurricane-new-orleans-refuse-evacuate-george-w-bush-home-piano-a8019586.html

CHAPTER 31. SOBER NOT SOBER

1. https://www.hope-rehab-center-thailand.com/king-baby-syndrome/

2. http://nymag.com/news/features/41007/

3. https://www.economist.com/prospero/2018/07/20/danny-fields-and-seymour-stein-champions-of-punk-look-back

4. https://www.nytimes.com/2007/11/01/nyregion/01murder.html?hp

5. https://www.telegraph.co.uk/news/worldnews/1568078/Linda-Stein-ex-Ramones-manager-murdered.html

6. https://nypost.com/2007/11/04/last-vow-of-top-broker/

7. https://www.nytimes.com/2010/02/24/nyregion/24stein.html

CHAPTER 32. MEMPHIS BLUES

1. Lisa is a dear friend I had known when she did publicity work for Elektra Records and Geffen Records. Lisa had picked up Cyndi as a client and referred me for A&R work.

2. https://www.advocate.com/music/2017/7/25/cyndi-lauper-when-things-get-really-bad-artists-respond

3. http://electraphonicrecording.com/

4. https://www.premierguitar.com/articles/20415-rig-rundown-jonny-lang

5. http://www.thecountryblues.com/artist-reviews/charlie-musselwhite-memphis-charlie/

6. https://www.theguardian.com/music/2015/nov/11/allen-toussaint

7. https://www.allmusic.com/artist/charles-skip-pitts-mn0000451317/biography

8. http://archive.commercialappeal.com/entertainment/stax-music-great-guitarist-charles-skip-pitts-dies-ep-386069037-324172411.html/

9. https://www.theguardian.com/music/2010/sep/30/cyndi-lauper-memphis-blues-cd-review

10. https://www.washingtonpost.com/blogs/local/wp/2014/05/16/a-one-woman-protest-at-the-lorraine-motel/?noredirect=on&utm_term=.87254b0dfd33

11. https://www.localmemphis.com/news/local-news/mlk50-room-306-at-the-lorraine-motel/953076942

12. https://www.nytimes.com/1988/03/03/us/eviction-empties-motel-where-dr-king-died.html

13. http://www.sebreephoto.com/copied-blog/2016/9/9/28-years-130-days-and
-counting

14. Dr. Martin Luther King, Jr., *Where Do We Go From Here: Chaos or Community?* (Boston: Beacon Press, 1967).

CHAPTER 33. NEVER FALL IN LOVE WITH A HOOKER

1. Excerpts from private journals. Author's collection.
2. https://www.imdb.com/name/nm1798128/bio?ref_=nm_dyk_qt_sm#quotes
3. *Ibid.*
4. https://www.nytimes.com/2013/03/25/sports/joe-weider-founder-of-a
-bodybuilding-empire-dies-at-93.html

CHAPTER 34. ROUGH GODS

1. https://www.zdnet.com/article/its-official-polaroid-will-stop-manufacturing
-instant-film-at-end-of-year/
2. https://us.polaroidoriginals.com/pages/about-us
3. https://wwd.com/eye/lifestyle/gallaghers-re-opens-in-partnership-with
-vfiles-5804364/
4. http://noize.buzz/Issues/cn52full.pdf

CHAPTER 35. WHO THE FUCK IS THAT GUY?

1. https://legendsarising.com/2012/08/31/review-xxx-all-ages-the-boston
-hardcore-film/
2. https://variety.com/2017/film/news/michael-alago-who-signed-metallica
-and-white-zombie-gets-the-documentary-treatment-in-who-the-fk-is-that
-guy-1202497423/

CHAPTER 36. BLANCHE

1. Anna Godbersen, *Splendor* (New York: HarperCollins, 2009).
2. https://www.mayoclinic.org/diseases-conditions/alzheimers-disease/expert-answers/sundowning/faq-20058511

CHAPTER 37. GRATITUDE

1. "The Serenity Prayer" by Reinhold Niebuhr.
2. A qualification is the speaker's personal story up to the point when they enter AA.
3. https://www.aa.org/assets/en_US/smf-121_en.pdf

INDEX